POSTCARDS
FROM THE '80S

POSTC

ARDS
from the '80s
80 LISTS
TO REMEMBER

edited by
Stephanie Bennett and Amy Hall

**Andrews McMeel
Publishing**

Kansas City

www.andrewsmcmeel.com

ISBN: 0-8362-9270-7

Library of Congress Catalog Card Number: 98:53692
  CIP data on file.

Designed by Holly Camerlinck

DEDICATIONS:

To the Shawnee Mission North High School
Class of 1988. And especially to Rich, my
fun husband, who, like me, never tires of
blasting Journey and tolerates my frequent
all-Rick Springfield music days with
remarkable patience.

--SB

For Scott, my hilarious husband, who is so
full of '80s trivia even Alex Trebek would
be impressed. And for my felines, Dante
and Emma, who assisted greatly with the
manuscript by shedding all over my desk,
attacking my pen, running away with my
posty-notes, and generally insisting that
I crack out the catnip instead.

--AH

CONTENTS

PREFACE

It all started with an innocent question posed to a group of friends over drinks: What was the best movie soundtrack of the '80s? The answers varied from person to person, but each was passionate about their personal choice. We had a blast debating and I vowed to listen to them all again.

My moonwalk through '80s nostalgia continued as I began to notice references to the decade everywhere. *The Wedding Singer*. MTV compilation CDs containing hits from each year. "You Know You're a Child of the '80s When . . . " E-mails. My ten-year high school reunion loomed. It seemed that you couldn't avoid the '80s. But then who would want to? It was such a fun, colorful, innocent decade. The music was synthetically fresh. The hair was big and stiff. The likes of John Cusack and Molly Ringwald ruled the silver screen. And there was massive shopping and arcade-game playing to be done at malls everywhere. It was a great decade to be a teenager.

All these signs pointed to the need for a collection of events, objects, fads, and people from the '80s to preserve the memories. That's what we've attempted to do in this homage to the supreme decade. The only rule about whether to include something or not was if it could be associated in any way with the years 1980 to 1989. We've tried to include as many perspectives as possible, but it would be impossible to catch every single thing. We beg for your forgiveness if we omitted something dear to your heart (or if someone you "love" landed in the "cheesy" category). Tell us what you think by contacting us at postcards@amuniversal.com We hope you enjoy reliving the memories even half as much as we enjoyed compiling them.

Remember: Never surrender, just say no, and walk like an Egyptian.

Stephanie Bennett

CONTRIBUTORS:

Rich Bennett
Stephanie Bennett
Polly Blair
Randall Blair
Bryan Camerlinck
Holly Camerlinck
Michelle Daniel
Nora Donaghy
Brad Fitz
Jennifer Fox
Kelly Gilbert
Amy Hall
JuJu Johnson

Tiffany Johnson
Jessica Kerrigan
Wade Kerrigan
Kris Koederitz
Geila Renard
Ron Renard
Patty Rice
Chris Schillig
Scott Shorter
Scott Wells
Kevin Worley
Jean Zevnik

ad campaigns, food,
cereal, words and phrases,
must-have magazines, books,
cartoons, toys, games, arcade
and video games, fitness,
sports teams and some of
their coaches, posters,
dating, birth control . . .

ENTERTAINMENT/LIFESTYLE of the '80s

ENTERTAINMENT/ LIFESTYLE

AIRMAIL

"Where's the Beef?"
and Other Ad Campaigns
Burned into Your Brain

"A pinch is all it takes!"
Skoal chewing tobacco

"Advanced Medicine for Pain"
Advil

"After all, if smoking isn't a pleasure, why bother? Alive with pleasure."
Newport cigarettes

American Tourister monkeys beating up luggage

"AT&T. The right choice."

"Beef. Real food for real people."

Bill Cosby for Jell-O

Blue-tinted, urban Levi's ads
with guys walking down
the street, giving a good view
of their "jeans"

"Can you tell which twin *didn't* just shampoo?"
Prell

"Clap on. Clap off. Clap on. Clap off. THE CLAPPER!"

"The Classic American Beauty"
Lauren by Ralph Lauren

"Come to think of it, I'll have a Heineken."

"Come to where the flavor is."
Philip Morris

Domino's Pizza's
Noid

"The Essence of Romance"
Le Jardin de Max Factor

Etonic.
Winning never felt better.

"Extra lasts
extra long."
Extra chewing gum

**"For lips he'll
take a shine to"**
L'Erin cosmetics

"The full-size napkin so thin
it fits in a wallet"
Sure & Natural Maxi Shield

"Gee Your Hair
Smells Terrific."

"Get a little taste of French culture."
Yopláit yogurt

"Get Met. It pays."
Snoopy for Metropolitan Life Insurance Co.

"Give me a light. I meant a Bud Light."

"Gulf people: Energy for tomorrow"
Gulf petroleum products

"Have you driven a Ford . . . lately?"

"I Heard It Through the Grapevine"
California Raisins

"Help! I've fallen and I can't get up!"

Medical alert product

Hertz commercials with O. J. Simpson running through airports

"Hey, kid. Catch."

Mean Joe Greene for Coca-Cola

"I bet he drinks Johnnie Walker."

"I dare you to knock this battery off my shoulder."

Everready batteries

"I'd Like to Teach the World to Sing"

(reprise) Coca-Cola

"'I don't fly airplanes. I fly people.' Frank Robinson, Captain."

American Airlines, Inc.

"I'm a Pepper, You're a Pepper"

Dr Pepper

"It's like having fresh panties all the time."
Carefree panty shields

"It's Spuds McKenzie, America's Party Animal."
Budweiser

"It's the right thing to do."
Quaker Oats Oatmeal

"I Want My MTV"
MTV

"Just Say No"
Nancy Reagan

"Know what I mean, Vern?"
Ernest, for milk

"Leave it to the minds of Minolta."

"Little. Yellow. Different. Better."
Nuprin

Max Headroom for diet Coke

Merle Norman's before and after
photos campaign

Michael Jackson catching on fire while shooting a Pepsi commercial

"Navy. It's not just a job, it's an adventure!"

"Nothing Beats a Great Pair of Legs"

L'eggs panty hose

"Oh what a feeling!"

Toyota

"Places to Go. Things to Do. Lee Jeans."

"Post Fruit & Fibre tastes so good you forget the fiber."

"Puts the power of the pros in your hands."
Raid

7UP's little red dots

"Share my secret for beautiful hair."
Jhirmack with Victoria Principal

"Still going"
Engergizer's pink bunny

"Strong enough for a man, but made for a woman."
Secret deodorant

"Tastes great, less filling"
Miller Lite

"Thank you for your support."
Bartles & Jaymes

"This is your brain on drugs"
Council for a Drug-Free America

"Two all-beef patties . . ."
McDonald's

"Underneath it's Bali."

"Volkswagen does it again."

"We bring revolution home."
Pioneer

"We run the tightest ship in the shipping business."
UPS

"When it absolutely positively has to be there overnight."
Federal Express

"When you shave with Daisy, you go a little crazy."
Gillette Daisy

"Where's the beef?"
Wendy's

"You asked for it, you got it."
Toyota

"You have my word on it."
and
"He's lying."
Isuzu

"You never forget your first girl."
St. Pauli Girl

Means of Nourishment:
Healthy vs. Tasty

Alfalfa sprouts

Bagels

Caprisun

Crystal Light

Frosted Mini-Wheats

Frozen yogurt with bad toppings mixed in

Granola snacks

Grapefruit

Juice boxes

Lite salad dressing explosion

Microwave popcorn
(depending on the level of butter)

Muffins

Oat bran

Raisins

Tofu

Water (designer bottles)

Yogurt

healthy.

junk food:
[i.e. Tasty]

Alcohol
Beef jerky
Big cookies
Boone's Farm wine
Bubble Yum
Charmkins candy
Cherry Coke
Chicken McNuggets
Coca-Cola Classic
Corona
Ding Dongs
Doritos
E.T. Candy
Fig Newtons
Fresca

Fruit Roll-Ups
Fruit Wrinkles
Fuzzy Navels
Gummi Bears
Ho Ho's
Jell-O Pudding Pops
Jeno's Pizza Rolls
Jiffy Pop
Jolly Rancher
Jolt Cola
Krunchers!
Little Debbie—
any of them
Lunchables
McD.L.T.

junk food: [i.e. Tasty]

McRibb
McSteak
Mello Yello
Microbrews
Miller High Life
Miller Lite
Mister Salty
Peanut butter M&M's
Nachos
New Coke
Pepsi
Pizza Hut
Pop Rocks
Pot pies

Powdered doughnuts
Reese's Pieces
Roller Racer chewing gum
Rolos
Star Wars cookies
Suicides (soda mixtures)
Tab
Teddy Grahams
Tostitos
Twinkies
Velveeta
What-cha-ma-call-it
Wine coolers

Every Kid's Favorite Part of Grocery Shopping with Mom:
The Cereal Aisle

BooBerry Cereal ○ Cap'n Crunch

Cinnamon Toast Crunch ○ Circus O's Cereal ○

Cocoa Pebbles ○ Cocoa Puffs ○ Cookie Crisps

Count Chocula Cereal ○ Cups and Cones Cereal

Frankenberry Cereal ○ Freaky's Cereal ○ Froot Loops

Fruit Islands Cereal

Fruity Pebbles ○ Ghost Busters Cereal ○

Honey Nut Cheerios

Lucky Charms ○ Mr. T Cereal ○ Nintendo Cereal

OJ's Cereal ○ Pac-Man Cereal

Strawberry Shortcake Cereal

Total ○ Trix ○ Waffelos

Yummy Mummy Cereal

Words and Phrases
you probably uttered at some point during the '80s

_____, not!

____, sucks!

Awesome

All-skate!

Babe

Bad

Barf-o-rama

Bodacious

Bogart

Bogus

Bitchin'

Burnout

Chick

Cowabunga

Cruise

DINK

Don't have a cow, man

Doozer

Dork

Downer

Dude

Duh!

Eat my shorts!

Excellent

Fer Shurrr

Gag me with a spoon

Geek

Gnarly

Grody

Grody to the max

I'm so sure

Jock

Jones

Like, _____ Killer

Mint

Neo-maxi zoom-dweebie

Oh my gawd!

Psyche! Preppie

Punk

Rad

Radical

Scarfing out

Skate

Snarf

So fine

Stoner

Sucks

Take a chill pill

Take off, eh!

That is *so* Joanie

Totally

Totally Tubular

To the max

Way, _____

What a stud muffin

Whatever

Word to your mother

Word up!

YO!

Yuppie

must-have
Magazines
We Grew Up Reading

**Bop • CoEd
Details • Dynamite • GQ
Hot Dog • MAD •
Picture Pages • Ranger Rick
Rolling Stone • Sassy
Seventeen • Spin
Sports Illustrated** (especially the swimsuit issue)
**• Teen • Teen Beat •
World • YM**

Tiger Beat

The Best-Selling and Most-Talked-About *Books* During the '80s

The Executioner's Song
Norman Mailer

The Official Preppy Handbook
Lisa Birnbach

101 Uses for a Dead Cat
Simon Bond

Noble House
James Clavell

Gorky Park
Martin Cruz Smith

Blubber
Judy Blume

The Beverly Hills Diet
Judy Mazel

Richard Simmons' Never-Say-Diet Book
Richard Simmons

Miss Piggy's Guide to Life
Miss Piggy as told to
Henry Beard

Dr. Atkins' Nutrition Breakthrough
Robert C. Atkins, M.D.

North and South
John Jakes

The Hotel New Hampshire
John Irving

Remembrance
Danielle Steel

Cujo
Stephen King

Jane Fonda's Workout Book
Jane Fonda

A Light in the Attic
Shel Silverstein

Choose Your Own Adventure books

When Bad Things Happen to Good People
Harold S. Kushner

The Lord God Made Them All
James Herriot

The Cinderella Complex
Colette Dowling

Real Men Don't Eat Quiche
Bruce Feirstein

Living, Loving & Learning
Leo Buscaglia

The One Minute Manager
Kenneth Blanchard and Spencer Johnson

Pet Sematary
Stephen King

Hollywood Wives
Jackie Collins

Motherhood: The Second Oldest Profession
Erma Bombeck

Bright Lights, Big City
Jay McInerney

Megatrends
John Naisbitt

The Hunt for Red October
Tom Clancy

If Tomorrow Comes
Sidney Sheldon

Iacocca: An Autobiography
Lee Iococca with
William Novak

Smart Women, Foolish Choices
Connell Cowan and
Melvyn Kinder

The Road Less Traveled
M. Scott Peck

The Handmaid's Tale
Margaret Atwood

Fatherhood
Bill Cosby

Enter Talking
Joan Rivers with
Richard Meryman

Skeleton Crew
Stephen King

The Color Purple
Alice Walker

Out of Africa
Isak Dinesen

Sniglets
Rich Hall

The Far Side Gallery
Gary Larson

It
Stephen King

The Prince of Tides
Pat Conroy

You're Only Old Once
Dr. Seuss

Men Who Hate Women and the Women Who Love Them
Susan Forward and Joan Torres

Outbreak
Robin Cook

The Clan of the Cave Bear
Jean M. Auel

Women Who Love Too Much
Robin Norwood

Adult Children of Alcoholics
Janet Geringer Woititz

The Bonfire of the Vanities
Tom Wolfe

Shining Through
Susan Isaacs

A Brief History of Time
Stephen W. Hawking

**The 8-Week
Cholesterol Cure**
Robert E. Kowalski

Patriot Games
Tom Clancy

Sphere
Michael Crichton

Presumed Innocent
Scott Turow

Small Sacrifices
Ann Rule

**Something Under the Bed
Is Drooling**
Bill Watterson

Tales from Margaritaville
Jimmy Buffett

**Oldest Living Confederate
Widow Tells All**
Allan Gurganus

Roseanne
by Roseanne Barr

**All I Really Need to Know I
Learned in Kindergarten**
Robert Fulghum

Martha Stewart's Christmas
Martha Stewart

While My Pretty One Sleeps
Mary Higgins Clark

'TOONS TO CATCH:

On a Saturday Morning, after School, or in the Paper

The Care Bears
Danger Mouse
Dilbert
Dungeons and Dragons
The Far Side
Fat Albert
Fonz and the Happy Days Gang
Foxtrot
G.I. Joe
Garfield

Baby Blues
Barbie and the Rockers
Battle of the Planets
Bloom County
The Bugaloos
Calvin and Hobbes
Captain Caveman
    and the Teen Angels

G-Force
Hanna-Barbera Cartoons,
    all of them
He-Man and the
    Masters of the Universe
Hong Kong Phooey
Inspector Gadget
It's Punky Brewster
Jabberjaw
The Jetsons
Josie and the Pussycats
The Looney Toons
The New Shmoo
The Rocky and
    Bullwinkle Show
Schoolhouse Rock
Scooby-Doo
Scooby's Laff-a-lympics
Shazam!

The Shirt Tales
Silver Hawks
The Simpsons
The Smurfs
The Snorks
Space Ghost and Dino Boy
Spider-Man
Strawberry Shortcake
Thundercats
The Transformers
Voltron
Wonder Woman
Woody Woodpecker
The World's Greatest
    Superfriends
X-Men
Yogi Bear
Ziggy

Cracking the Cube:

GAME$

from an '80s Childhood

Battleship

Boggle

Chutes and Ladders

Clue

Connect 4

Electronic Battleship

Headache

Hungry, Hungry Hippos

Life

Mastermind

Monopoly

Mousetrap

Operation

Othello

Pente

Pictionary

Pizza Party

Rubik's Cube

Sorry!

Trivial Pursuit

Uno

Yahtzee

Even If *You* Didn't Have These
TOYS,
Chances Are Some Kid in Your Neighborhood *Did*

· Atari · Baby Alive · Barbie ·

· Big Wheel · BMX Hard Tail Bicycles ·

· Cabbage Patch Kids (and Garbage Pail Kids) ·

· Care Bears · Chinese Jumprope ·

· Cliff Hangers racing sets · Construx · Cricket ·

· Crystar · Easy-Bake Toys ·

· Garfield anything · G.I. Joe · Glo Worm Light & Learn ·

· Go Bots · Green Machine · Hello Kitty ·

· Hot Wheels and orange plastic race tracks ·

· Lego Toys · Lincoln Logs · Lite-Brite · M.A.S.K. toys ·

· Madballs · Mangloids · Micro Machines ·

· Monchhichis · Muppet Babies · M.U.S.C.L.E. Toys ·

· My Buddy/Kid Sister · My Little Pony · My Pet Monster ·

· Ninja Toys · Paddington Bear · PogoBall ·

· Pop Wheels (combination tennis shoe and roller skate) ·

Popples Toys · Pound Puppies · The Puffalumps ·

Rainbow Brite · Rubik's Cube · She-ra Dolls · Shrinky Dinks ·

· Sit 'n Spin · Skateboards · Slinky ·

· Snoopy plush toy (and all his little coordinated outfits) ·

· Snoopy Sno Cone machines · Speak & Spell ·

· Star Wars figures (all of them) ·

· Stickers and sticker albums · Stomper 4x4s ·

· Strawberry Shortcake · Stretch Armstrong ·

· Super Balls · Teddy Ruxpin ·

· Teenage Mutant Ninja Turtles · Transformers ·

· Wacky Wallwalkers

Neighborhood
GAMES

(when it was still safe to play outside at night)

Capture the Flag

Flashlight Tag

Ghost in the Graveyard

Hide and Seek

Wiffle Ball

Danger Toys

(we're lucky we lived through childhood)

Asphalt underneath equipment
(not soft wood chips)

Baby walkers

Big Wheels

Cribs with nonstandard slats

Easy-Bake Toys

Green Machine

Hooded sweatshirts
(those ties will strangle you!)

Lawn Jarts

Merry-go-round or a bucking horse in
McDonald's (no safe playlands
or Discovery Zones)

Metal playground equipment
(not recycled plastic or wood)

Metal slides with screws poking up

Power Wheels (battery-powered, full-size
toy cars that spontaneously caught on fire—
Barbie Jeep, Big Jake, Extreme Machine)

Swings with chains, not ropes

Where Our Quarters Went:
ARCADE AND VIDEO GAMES

Asteroids

Battle Zone

Berzerk

Bump-N-Jump

Burgertime

Centipede

Defender

Dig Dug

Donkey Kong

Donkey Kong Junior

Dragon's Lair

Frogger

Galaga

Gauntlet

Gorf

I, Robot

Joust

JumpMan Junior

Lunar Lander

M.A.C.H. 3

Mad Planets

Mario Bros.

Millipede

Missile Command

Ms. Pac-Man

Pac-Man

Pitfall

Pole Position

Pong

Q*bert

Qix

Quantam

Robotron: 2084

Space Ace

Space Harrier

Stargate

Star Wars

S.T.U.N. Runner

Tempest 2000

Tron

Xevious

Zaxxon

Atari games

Adventure
Asteroids
Barnstorming
Beany Bopper

Bermuda Triangle
Berzerk
BMX Airmaster
Centipede
Chopper Command
Combat

Defender
Demon Attack
Donkey Kong
Enduro
Frogger
Frostbite

Haunted House
HERO
Indy 500
Kaboom

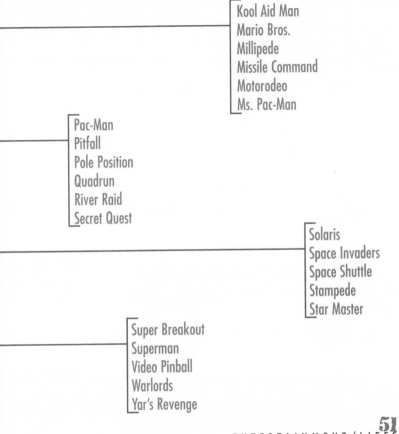

Kool Aid Man
Mario Bros.
Millipede
Missile Command
Motorodeo
Ms. Pac-Man

Pac-Man
Pitfall
Pole Position
Quadrun
River Raid
Secret Quest

Solaris
Space Invaders
Space Shuttle
Stampede
Star Master

Super Breakout
Superman
Video Pinball
Warlords
Yar's Revenge

the fitness CRAZE
of the '80s was manifested in:

Aerobics kills, uh sweeps, nation

Aerobics shows on TV at all times
of the day and night

Dawn of the home-exercise video collection

Deal-a-Meal

Gym memberships
(had to have one to be cool)

Jane Fonda declared workout guru

Jazzercize

Jogging

NordicTrack

Race walking

Richard Simmons' videos

Running

Soloflex

Step aerobics

Strap-on ankle weights for walking

Tennis

ThighMaster—Suzanne Somers

Sports Dynasties:

Boston Celtics

Edmonton Oilers

Los Angeles Lakers

New York Islanders

Oakland A's

Oakland/Los Angeles Raiders

San Francisco 49ers

Bitter Rivalries:

Cardinals versus Cubs

Dodgers versus Yankees

Lakers versus Celtics

HIGH-PROFILE COACHES

Bobby Bowden	Tony LaRussa
Scotty Bowman	Tommy Lasorda
Larry Brown	Tom Osborne
Mike Ditka	Bill Parcells
Whitey Herzog	Pat Riley
Lou Holtz	Dean Smith
Jimmy Johnson	John Thompson
Bobby Knight	Jim Valvano
Tom Landry	Bill Walsh

We are the Champions

Champions
World Series Winners

Philadelphia Phillies	**(1980)**
Los Angeles Dodgers	**(1981)**
St. Louis Cardinals	**(1982)**
Baltimore Orioles	**(1983)**
Detroit Tigers	**(1984)**
Kansas City Royals	**(1985)**
New York Mets	**(1986)**
Minnesota Twins	**(1987)**
Los Angeles Dodgers	**(1988)**
Oakland A's	**(1989)**

57

We are the
Champions

Super Bowl Winners

Pittsburgh Steelers	**(1980)**
Oakland Raiders	**(1981)**
San Francisco 49ers	**(1982)**
Washington Redskins	**(1983)**
Los Angeles Raiders	**(1984)**
San Francisco 49ers	**(1985)**
Chicago Bears	**(1986)**
New York Giants	**(1987)**
Washington Redskins	**(1988)**
San Francisco 49ers	**(1989)**

NOW-DEFUNCT
Sports Teams
from the '80s

St. Louis Cardinals (football)
Baltimore Colts (football)
Minnesota North Stars (hockey)
Kansas City Kings (basketball)
New Orleans Jazz (basketball)
Atlanta Flames (hockey)
Denver Rockies (hockey)
Los Angeles Raiders (football)

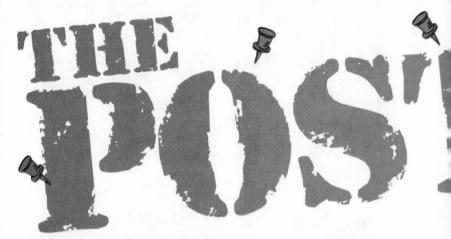

THE POST

That Covered the Walls, Closet Doors,

60 POSTCARDS FROM THE '80S

ERS
and Ceilings
of Our Youth

Paula Abdul   Bryan Adams

Anonymous shirtless
Soloflex stud

Catherine Bach as Daisy Duke

Scott Baio   Jason Bateman

Justine Bateman

Jon Bon Jovi

Christie Brinkley

Kirk Cameron   The Cars

David Cassidy

Shaun Cassidy

Cathy Lee Crosby

Tom Cruise Beverly D'Angelo

Johnny Depp Donna Dixon

Duran Duran Emilio Estevez

Michael J. Fox

Farrah Fawcett Andy Gibb

The Go-Go's

Anthony Michael Hall

The Hardy Boys

Corey Hart

Kathy Ireland

Don Johnson   Howard Jones
Tawny Kitaen
Lorenzo Lamas
Heather Locklear   Chad Lowe
Rob Lowe   Ralph Macchio
Elle Macpherson
Madonna   Kristy McNichol
Menudo
Demi Moore   Judd Nelson
New Kids on the Block
Markie Post
Ricky Schroder

Tom Selleck   Brooke Shields

Elisabeth Shue

Rick Springfield   John Stamos

Star Wars, especially
Harrison Ford

Mr. T   Heather Thomas

Phillip Michael Thomas

Cheryl Tiegs

John Travolta

Jack Wagner

Lisa Whelchel

"The next skate is for couples only": things to do on a date

Amusement park

Mall strolling

Miniature golf

Parking

Arcade

Cruising

Group dates

Concerts

Party at the absent-parent house

Pizza joint, just hang out

Make out at the park
(or anywhere for that matter)

Rent a movie

Roller-skating

Skate party
("This is an all-skate!")

School games:
football,
basketball,
volleyball,
soccer, or
baseball

School dances

Fifth quarters at the church

Getting frozen yogurt

Record a song
together at the mall

Things That Served as
Birth Control

Watching the Reagans together

Watching Fatal Attraction

Watching 8 is Enough

Pocket protectors

The Pill

Parents who never traveled or left the house

Living at home

Listening to "Papa Don't Preach"

Homes without a basement or rumpus room

Herpes, HIV (just name your sexually transmitted disease of choice)

Early withdrawal

Early curfews

Diaphragm

Condoms

Backseat of a Vega

Aspirin held between the knees

Abstention (yeah, right)

USE COIN TO SET STARTING DAY

SUN MON TUE WED THU FRI SAT

THESE PEOPLE, EVENTS, AND THINGS JUST SCREAM

"*Total Cheese!*"

Airplane! and *Airplane 2: The Sequel*

Beauty and the Beast (TV)

Beetlejuice

The Blue Lagoon

Breakin' and *Breakin' 2: Electric Boogaloo*

Cheech and Chong

Desperately Seeking Susan

Dirty Dancing
(Patrick Swayze in particular)

Early MTV videos
(think paint splatters and strobe lights)

"Escape
(The Piña Colada Song)"

Fantasy Island

The Goonies

Gremlins

Hands Across America

Hard to Hold,
Rick Springfield's movie masterpiece

Howard the Duck

Hulk Hogan

"The Humpty Dance"
by Digital Underground

Karate Kid movies (all of them!)

"Karma Chameleon"
by Culture Club

Joanie Loves Chachi

The Love Boat

Mannequin

Ed McMahon ("Yes!")

Police Academy
(in all its incarnations)

Porky's

David Lee Roth

Richard Simmons

Solid Gold and the *Solid Gold* dancers

Star Search

"Superbowl Shuffle"
by the Chicago Bears Shufflin' Crew

Teen Wolf

Top Secret!

Velveeta (of course)

"We Are the World" footage of the
recording of the song

Chuck Woolery
(*Love Connection* host)

the bands—including girl bands, makeup bands, hair bands, unique band names, solo singers, grammy winners, soundtracks, flashback tunes, one-hit wonders . . .

MUSIC of the '80s

MUSIC

AIRMAIL

Bitchin' **Bands** from the '80s

ABC

AC/DC

Adam Ant

Aerosmith

a-ha

Air Supply

Alabama

Alan Parsons Project

Animotion

Asia

The Bangles

The Beastie Boys

Berlin

The B-52s

Big Country

Blondie

Bon Jovi

The Boomtown Rats

Boston

Breathe

John Cafferty & Beaver Brown Band

The Cars

77 MUSIC

Cheap Trick

Chicago

Cinderella

The Clash

The Commodores

Christopher Cross

Crowded House

Culture Club

The Cure

Cutting Crew

The Charlie Daniels Band

Morris Day and the Time

Dead Or Alive

Debarge

Def Leppard

Depeche Mode

Devo

Dire Straits

DJ Jazzy Jeff and the Fresh Prince

Dokken

Duran Duran

79 MUSIC

Echo and the Bunnymen

EMF

The Eurythmics

Fabulous Thunderbirds

The Fixx

Fleetwood Mac

Foreigner

Frankie Goes to Hollywood

J. Geils Band

Genesis

Glass Tiger

The Go-Go's

Golden Earring

Guns n' Roses

Hall and Oates

Jeff Healey Band

Heart

The Honeydrippers

The Hooters

81
MUSIC

The Human League

INXS

The Jets

Journey

Kajagoogoo

Katrina and the Waves

Greg Kihn Band

The Kinks

Kiss

Kool and the Gang

Level 42

Huey Lewis and the News

Little River Band

Los Lobos

Loverboy

Madness

Menudo

Men At Work

Men Without Hats

Metallica

Miami Sound Machine

Steve Miller Band

83 MUSIC

1
(20:11)

Milli Vanilli

Modern English

The Motels

Mötley Crüe

Mr. Mister

Naked Eyes

New Edition

New Kids on the Block

New Order

Night Ranger

Noise

Nu Shooz

Oak Ridge Boys

Oingo Boingo

Orchestral Manoeuvres in the Dark (OMD)

The Outfield

The Pet Shop Boys

Tom Petty and the Heartbreakers

Pink Floyd

Pointer Sisters

Poison

The Police

Power Station

The Pretenders

85 MUSIC

Prince and the Revolution

The Psychedelic Furs

Quarterflash

Queen

Quiet Riot

Ratt

Ready for the World

R.E.M.

REO Speedwagon

Restless Heart

The Rolling Stones

The Romantics

Run-D.M.C.

Scorpions

Scritti Politti

Bob Seger and the Silver Bullet Band

The Sex Pistols

Sheriff

Simple Minds

The Smiths

The Smithereens

Spandau Ballet

Bruce Springsteen and the E Street Band

Starship

The Stray Cats

Stryper

Styx

Survivor

Talking Heads

Tears for Fears

.38 Special

The Thompson Twins

George Thorogood and the Destroyers

Toto

The Traveling Wilburys

The Tubes

Twisted Sister

UB40

U2

Van Halen
(with David Lee Roth, then with Sammy Hagar)

Violent Femmes

Wang Chung

Warrant

Wham!

Winger

Yaz

Yes

ZZ Top

89 MUSIC

Girls Just Wanna Have Fun
Great Girl Bands and Singers

Paula Abdul **Anita Baker** *Bananarama*

The Bangles *Toni Basil* **Pat Benatar**

The B-52s **Blondie** *Laura Branigan*

Irene Cara *Belinda Carlisle* **Kim Carnes**

Taylor Dayne **Sheena Easton**

Gloria Estefan **Exposé** *Debbie Gibson*

The Go-Go's *Heart* **Whitney Houston**

Janet Jackson **The Jets**
Joan Jett and the Blackhearts
Chaka Khan Cyndi Lauper
Annie Lennox
Lisa Lisa and Cult Jam **Madonna**
The Motels **Juice Newton**
Olivia Newton-John
Stevie Nicks The Pointer Sisters **Sade**
Donna Summer **Tiffany** Tina Turner
Bonnie Tyler Jody Wattey
Wendy and Lisa Wilson Phillips

91 MUSIC

Cosmetically

Adam Ant

David Bowie

Alice Cooper

Culture Club

The Cure

Dead or Alive

Depeche Mode

Duran Duran

A Flock of Seagulls

King

Enhanced Bands

IN TRUE '80S STYLE

Kiss

Modern English

Mötley Crüe

Pet Shop Boys

Poison

Prince and the Revolution

The Romantics

The Smiths

The Thompson Twins

Twisted Sister

BANDS WHO PROUDLY TOOK THEIR HAIR TO
New Heights

Anthrax	Great White	Mötley Crüe	Van Halen (SELECT MEMBERS)
Bon Jovi	Guns n' Roses	Night Ranger	Warrant
Bulletboys	Heart	Poison	"Weird Al" Yankovic
Cinderella	Iron Maiden	Quiet Riot	Wham!
The Cult	Judas Priest	Ratt	White Lion
The Cure	Kingdom Come	Scorpions	Whitesnake
Damn Yankees	Kiss	Sheriff	Winger
Def Leppard	L.A. Guns	Skid Row	ZZ Top (AND BEARD BAND)
Dokken	Cyndi Lauper	Slaughter	
Eurythmics	Loverboy	Stryper	
Faster Pussycat	Megadeth	The Thompson Twins	
A Flock of Seagulls	Metallica	Twisted Sister	

What's a Kajagoogoo?:

Uniquely '80s Band Names

a-ha • Bananarama • The B-52s • Bow Wow Wow
• The Buggles • The Cult •
• Dexy's Midnight Runners •
• Echo and the Bunnymen •
• Ethel & the Shameless Hussys •
• Frankie Goes to Hollywood •
Haircut 100 • The Hooters • Johnny Hates Jazz
• Kajagoogoo • Naked Eyes • Oingo Boingo •
• Orchestral Manoeuvres in the Dark (OMD) •
• The Outfield • Quiet Riot •
Siouxsie and the Banshees • Spandau Ballet
• Wang Chung • Yello •

totally awesome
SOLO singers

Paula Abdul ★ Bryan Adams

John Anderson ★ Adam Ant

Rob Base ★ Toni Basil

Pat Benatar ★ Clint Black

Blondie ★ David Bowie

Boy George ★ Bobby Brown

Jackson Browne ★ Irene Cara

Belinda Carlisle ★ Cher

Eric Clapton ★ Phil Collins

Elvis Costello ★ Christopher Cross

Terence Trent D'Arby ★ Dennis DeYoung

Paul Davis ★ Kool Moe Dee

Neil Diamond ★ Thomas Dolby ★ Shelia E.

Sheena Easton ★ Gloria Estefan

Falco ★ Dan Fogelberg

John Fogerty ★ Lita Ford

Samantha Fox ★ Glenn Frey

Peter Gabriel ★ Crystal Gayle

Debbie Gibson ★ Amy Grant ★ Eddy Grant

Sammy Hagar ★ M.C. Hammer

Herbie Hancock ★ Corey Hart

Don Henley ★ Whitney Houston

Billy Idol ★ James Ingram

Janet Jackson ★ Jermaine Jackson

Joe Jackson ★ Michael Jackson

97 MUSIC

Rick James ★ Billy Joel

Elton John ★ Don Johnson

Howard Jones ★ Chaka Khan

Kris Kristofferson ★ Cyndi Lauper ★ Julian Lennon

L.L. Cool J. ★ Tone-Lōc ★ Kenny Loggins

Madonna ★ Richard Marx

Paul McCartney ★ John Cougar Mellencamp

George Michael ★ Eddie Money ★ Alannah Myles

Nena ★ Olivia Newton-John

Aldo Nova ★ Billy Ocean

Jeffrey Osborne ★ Ozzy Osbourne

Robert Palmer (and all those clone chicks!)

Ray Parker Jr. ★ Dolly Parton

Sandi Patti ★ Steve Perry

Prince ★ Eddie Rabbitt

Lionel Richie ★ Kenny Rogers

David Lee Roth ★ Paul Simon

Patty Smyth ★ Rick Springfield

Bruce Springsteen ★ Billy Squier

Rod Stewart ★ Sting

George Strait ★ Tiffany

Randy Travis ★ Tina Turner

Vanilla Ice ★ Vanity

Stevie Ray Vaughan ★ John Waite

Kim Wilde ★ Hank Williams Jr.

Bruce Willis ★ Steve Winwood

Stevie Wonder ★ "Weird Al" Yankovic

Dwight Yoakam ★ Paul Young

Young MC

Grammy Winners

1980

Record of the Year:
Sailing by Christopher Cross
New Artist: Christopher Cross

1981

Record of the Year:
Bette Davis Eyes by Kim Carnes
New Artist: Sheena Easton

1982

Record of the Year:
Rosanna by Toto
New Artist: Men At Work

1983

Record of the Year:
Beat It by Michael Jackson
New Artist: Culture Club

1984

Record of the Year:
What's Love Got to Do with It by Tina Turner
New Artist: Cyndi Lauper

1985

Record of the Year:
We Are the World by USA for Africa
New Artist: Sade

1986

Record of the Year: *Higher Love* by Steve Winwood
New Artist: Bruce Hornsby and the Range

1987

Record of the Year:
Graceland by Paul Simon
New Artist: Jody Watley

1988

Record of the Year:
Don't Worry Be Happy by Bobby McFerrin
New Artist: Tracy Chapman

1989

Record of the Year:
Wind Beneath My Wings by Bette Midler
New Artist: Milli Vanilli (which was later taken
away when their charade was exposed)

101
MUSIC

TOTALLY HOT Movie Soundtracks

Batman

Beverly Hills Cop

The Big Chill

Blade Runner

The Blues Brothers

Dirty Dancing

Eddie and the Cruisers

Fame

Flashdance

Footloose

The Lost Boys

Miami Vice

Pretty in Pink

Purple Rain

Say Anything

Some Kind of Wonderful

St. Elmo's Fire

Streets of Fire

Top Gun

Urban Cowboy

Vision Quest

Xanadu (double album)

Yentl

SONGS GUARANTEED TO GIVE YOU AN '80s Flashback

"Always Something There to Remind Me"
Naked Eyes

"Beat It"
Michael Jackson

"Be Good to Yourself"
Journey

"Billie Jean"
Michael Jackson

"Break My Stride"
Matthew Wilder

"Can't Fight This Feeling"
REO Speedwagon

"Come On Eileen"
Dexy's Midnight Runners

"Crazy for You"
Madonna

"Dancing with Myself"
Billy Idol

"Der Kommissar"
After the Fire

"Don't Worry Be Happy"
Bobby McFerrin

"Don't You Want Me"
The Human League

"Do They Know It's Christmas"
Band Aid

"Do You Believe in Love"
Huey Lewis and the News

"Do You Really Want to Hurt Me"
Culture Club

"867-5309/Jenny"
Tommy Tutone

"Electric Avenue"
Eddy Grant

"Everytime You Go Away"
Paul Young

"Forever Young"
Alphaville

"Freeze-Frame"
J. Geils Band

"Girls Just Wanna Have Fun"
Cyndi Lauper

"Goodbye to You"
Scandal

"Here I Go Again"
Whitesnake

"Hold Me Now"
The Thompson Twins

"Hold On Loosely"
.38 Special

"Human Touch"
Rick Springfield

"Hungry Like the Wolf"
Duran Duran

"I Can't Drive 55"
Sammy Hagar

"If You Leave"
Orchestral Manoeuvres in the Dark (OMD)

"(I Just) Died in Your Arms"
Cutting Crew

"I Melt with You"
Modern English

"I Ran (So Far Away)"
Flock of Seagulls

"I Want a New Drug"
Huey Lewis and the News

"Jack and Diane"
John Cougar Mellencamp

"Jesse's Girl"
Rick Springfield

"Karma Chameleon"
Culture Club

"Kyrie"
Mr. Mister

"Let's Go Crazy"
Prince

"Lick It Up"
Kiss

"Like A Virgin"
Madonna

"Little Red Corvette"
Prince

"Mickey"
Toni Basil

"Modern Love"
David Bowie

"1999"
Prince

"99 Luftballoons"
Nena

"No One Is to Blame"
Howard Jones

"No Parking on the Dance Floor"
Midnight Star

"One More Night"
Phil Collins

"One Night in Bangkok"
Murray Head

"Open Arms"
Journey

"Our House"
Madness

"Physical"
Olivia Newton John

"Purple Rain"
Prince

109 MUSIC

"The Reflex"
Duran Duran

"Rock Me Amadeus"
Falco

"Rock This Town"
The Stray Cats

"The Rose"
Bette Midler

"Safety Dance"
Men Without Hats

"Sara"
Starship

"She Blinded Me with Science"
Thomas Dolby

"She Drives Me Crazy"
Fine Young Cannibals

"Shout"
Tears for Fears

"Sister Christian"
Night Ranger

"Somebody's Watching Me"
Rockwell

"Something So Strong"
Crowded House

"Strip"
Adam Ant

"Summer of '69"
Bryan Adams

"Super Freak"
Rick James

"Sussudio"
Phil Collins

"Tainted Love"
Soft Cell

"Take My Breath Away"
Berlin

"Take On Me"
a-ha

111
MUSIC

"Things Can Only Get Better"
Howard Jones

"Thriller"
Michael Jackson

"True"
Spandau Ballet

"U Got the Look"
Prince and Sheena Easton

"Video Killed the Radio Star"
The Buggles

"Wake Me Up Before You Go Go"
Wham!

"We Are the World"
USA for Africa

"We Got the Beat"
The Go-Go's

"You Spin Me Round Round"
Dead or Alive

And Then There Was Silence . . .

One-Hit Wonders from the '80s

"Axel F".	Harold Faltemeyer
"Breakin'"	**Ollie and Jerry**
"Break My Stride"	Matthew Wilder
"Bust a Move"	**Young MC**
"Come on Eileen"	Dexy's Midnight Runners
"The Curly Shuffle"	**Jump 'n the Saddle Band**
"Der Kommissar"	After the Fire
"Don't Worry Be Happy"	**Bobby McFerrin**
"867-5309/Jenny"	Tommy Tutone
"Election Day"	**Arcadia**
"Far from Over"	Frank Stallone
"Forever Young"	**Alphaville**

"Perfect Way". . . . . Scritti Politti
"The Promise" . . . . **When in Rome**
"Puttin' on the Ritz" . . . . Taco
"The Rain". . . . . **Oran "Juice" Jones**
"Relax". . . . . Frankie Goes to Hollywood
"Rock Me Amadeus". . . . . **Falco**
"Rock On" . . . . Michael Damian
"Rumors" . . . . **Timex Social Club**
"Stars on 45" . . . . Stars on 45
"Tainted Love". . . . . **Soft Cell**
"Take Off". . . . . Bob and Doug McKenzie
"Take On Me". . . . . **a-ha**
"Tarzan Boy". . . . . Baltimora
"Tender Love" . . . . **Force M.D.'s**
"Tenderness" . . . . General Public
"Too Shy" . . . . **Kajagoogoo**
"Two of Hearts" . . . . Stacey Q
"Video Killed the Radio Star". . . . . . . **The Buggles**
"Voices Carry" . . . . 'Til Tuesday
"We Are the World". . . . . **USA for Africa**
"Wild, Wild West". . . . . Escape Club

Song Lyrics:

Now That You're in the Swing of Things, Can You Guess These Song Titles and Artists? *(Answers are on page 121)*

1 *And there's a heart that's breaking down this long-distance line tonight*

2 *Bermuda, Bahama, come on pretty mama*

3 *Blew out the speakers in her daddy's radio*

4 *Dearly beloved, we are gathered here today to get through this thing called life*

5 *Every time you call my name, I heat up like a burnin' flame*

6 *Goddess on the mountain top*

7 *He just smiled and gave me a vegamite sandwich*

8 *Her hair reminds me of a warm soft place where as a child I'd lie*

9 *Hop in my Chrysler it's as big as a whale and it's about to set sail*

10 *I am the maker of rules, dealing with fools*

11 *I feel so dirty when they start talking cute, I wanna tell her that I love her but the point is probly moot*

12 *If you want to find all the cops they're hanging out in the donut shop*

13 *I got in a little hometown jam, so they put a rifle in my hands*

14 *I got it, I got it, I got your number on the wall*

15 *I got my first real six-string, at the five and dime*

16 *I know when to pull you closer, and I know when to let you loose*

17 *I need fifty dollars to make you holler*

18 *In my mind and in my car, I can't rewind I've gone too far*

19 *It must've been some kind of kiss, I should've walked away*

20 *It's gonna take money, a whole lotta spendin' money*

21 *I've done no harm, I keep to myself, there's nothing wrong with my state of mental health*

22 *I've got my back against the record machine*

23 *I've seen a million faces, and I've rocked them all*

24 *I was standing, you were there, two worlds collided*

25 *Let me hear your body talk*

26 *My heart will break, I have loved you for so long. It's all I can take*

27 *No huggin' no kissin' til I get a wedding ring*

28 *Out on the road today I saw a deadhead sticker on a Cadillac*

29 *Put another dime in the juke box, baby*

30 *Rolling like thunder, under the covers*

31 *Ronny, Bobby, Ricky and Mike, if I like a girl who cares who you like*

32 *She had the body of a Venus, Lord imagine my surprise*

33 *Sister's sighing in her sleep*

34 *Streetlight people, living just to find emotion*

35 *Suckin' on chili dogs outside the Tastee-Freeze*

36 *The five years we have had have been such good times*

37 *There is freedom within, there is freedom without*

38 *There's a skeleton chokin' on a crust of bread*

39 *The road is long, there are mountains in our way*

40 *To see her in that negligee is really just too much*

41 *Troubled times, caught between confusion and pain*

42 *Wet bus stop, she's waiting, my car is warm and dry*

43 *Wheel of Fortune, Sally Ride, Heavy Metal, Suicide, Foreign debts, Homeless Vets, AIDS, Crack, Bernie Goetz*

44 *Work all day, to earn his pay, so we can play all night*

45 *You see it all around you, good lovin' gone bad*

46 *You take me by the heart and you take me by the hand*

Song Lyrics Answers

1 "Missing You," John Waite
2 "Kokomo," Beach Boys
3 "Shakin'," Eddie Money
4 "Let's Go Crazy," Prince
5 "Abracadabra," Steve Miller Band
6 "She's Got It," Bananarama
7 "Down Under," Men At Work
8 "Sweet Child o' Mine," Guns n' Roses
9 "Love Shack," The B-52s
10 "Eye in the Sky," Alan Parsons Project
11 "Jesse's Girl," Rick Springfield
12 "Walk Like an Egyptian," The Bangles
13 "Born in the U.S.A.," Bruce Springsteen
14 "867-5309/Jenny," Tommy Tutone
15 "Summer of '69," Bryan Adams
16 "Making Love Out of Nothing at All," Air Supply
17 "Wild Thing," Tone Lōc
18 "Video Killed the Radio Star," The Buggles
19 "(I Just) Died in Your Arms," Cutting Crew
20 "Got My Mind Set on You," George Harrison
21 "Who Can It Be Now?" Men At Work
22 "Jump," Van Halen

23 "Wanted Dead or Alive," Bon Jovi
24 "Never Tear Us Apart," INXS
25 "Physical," Olivia Newton-John
26 "Don't Forget Me When I'm Gone," Glass Tiger
27 "Keep Your Hands to Yourself," Georgia Satellites
28 "The Boys of Summer," Don Henley
29 "I Love Rock 'n Roll," Joan Jett and the Blackhearts
30 "I Guess That's Why They Call It the Blues," Elton John
31 "Cool It Now," New Edition
32 "Dude (Looks Like a Lady)," Aerosmith
33 "Our House," Madness
34 "Don't Stop Believing," Journey
35 "Jack and Diane," John Cougar Mellencamp
36 "Don't You Want Me," Human League
37 "Don't Dream It's Over," Crowded House
38 "King of Pain," The Police
39 "Up Where We Belong," Joe Cocker and Jennifer Warens
40 "Centerfold," J. Geils Band
41 "Separate Ways (Worlds Apart)," Journey
42 "Don't Stand So Close to Me," The Police
43 "We Didn't Start the Fire," Billy Joel
44 "Morning Train," Sheena Easton
45 "Hold On Loosely," .38 Special
46 "Mickey," Toni Basil

"bigger is better," fads, fashion designers, big hair secrets, jeans, "Material Girl" styles, shoes, love scents, beauty products . . .

FASHION/TRENDS of the '80s

FASHION/
TRENDS

Things that Capture the '80s "Bigger Is Better" Attitude:

Bags
Belts
Big Gulps from QuikTrip
Boom boxes
Breast implants
Calories
Cookies
Defense budgets
Earrings

Fat boys (Louie Anderson, "Refrigerator" Perry)
Hair
High heels
Huge hair bows/accessories
Monster trucks
Movie budgets
Multiplex theaters were born
Population of the planet hit five billion people in 1987
RJR Nabisco bought out for twenty-five billion dollars
Satellite dishes
Shoulder pads
Sneakers for men
Stereo speakers
Tires on trucks
United States' first trillion-dollar budget is passed
Wal-Mart explosion
Workout wardrobe

Fads and Crazes from the '80s

Aerobics/working out

Atari

Attending *The Rocky Horror Picture Show* armed with props

"Baby on Board" signs

Big cookies

Black light posters

"Boom boxes" with cassettes

The Brat Pack

Breakdancing

Cabbage Patch Kids

"Cause" songs

Colleco

Collectible Smurfs

Commodore 64

Decorating with geese figurines, and then cows

Drum machines

E.T.

Fiber-optic lamps sold at

Spencer's, with neon tips that swayed
Flashdance look
Garfield anything, but especially plush Garfields
   suction-cupped in car windows
Gnomes
Greed
   Alex Keaton (Michael J. Fox) on *Family Ties*
   DINKs
   Reganomics
   Wall Street
   Yuppies
Gremlins
Izod shirts
Laser Tag
Lip synching
Lunch box themes (plastic boxes, not metal)
   Pigs in Space
   Night Rider
   Raiders of the Lost Ark
   Scooby-Doo
   Star Wars
   Strawberry Shortcake

Madonna wanna-bes
Moonwalking
Neon colors
Nintendo
Paint splatter look
Pastel colors, think *Miami Vice* style and
    Chuck Taylor shoes
Ramp skating and Skateboarding
Rubik's Cubes
Sneaking a Stephen King book under the covers
Tanning beds
3-D revival *(Jaws)*
Trampolines
Trapper Keeper notebooks
Trick bike riders
Valley Girls
Vogueing
The Wave at sporting events
WWF wrestling (when people thought it was real)
Windbreakers that folded into their front pocket
    and then belted around your waist for convenience

The Clothing Designers and Brands That Said
"Fashion!"

Benetton	Ralph Lauren
Camp Beverly Hills	Members Only
Esprit	Mia
Gloria Vanderbilt	Ocean Pacific
Gucci	Pepe
Guess?	Sergio Valente
Halston	Swatch
Izod	Tommy Hilfiger
Jordache	Vans
Calvin Klein	Vuarnet
LaCoste	

Fashionable *Babes* of the Decade Sported...

All black with pale makeup

Baby pink

Baggy jeans and tops

Bangles

Beaded twist necklaces

Belted shirts

Blue eyeliner

Big belts and double-wrap belts

Big bows on blouses

Big, colorful earrings

Boxer shorts as shorts

Buttons on jackets (the more the merrier)

Collars up

Cardigans

Corduroy

Eastlands

Drop-waist dresses

Florescent-colored clothing

Friendship pins

Jams

Jean jackets and skirts

Jelly bracelets

Hawaiian prints/leis

Layers (two T-shirts with sleeves rolled up together)

Leggings

Leg warmers

Makeup, way too much

Metallic gold or silver bags and shoes

Midriff-revealing tees

Moccasins

Net vests

Neon anything

Opaque panty hose

Overalls

Pants, tiny at the ankles

Pins at collar

Pumps

Shaker sweaters

Shirt tails out

Shorts like those in Dirty Dancing, cuffed cut-off jeans

Shorts over sweatpants

Shoulder pads (huge)

Socks outside jeans

Soft, fuzzy, angora sweaters in pastel colors

Stirrup pants with heels

Swatch watches

Sweatshirts inside out

Sweatshirts ripped up

Triangular look (big at the shoulders and tapering to a point at the feet)

Turquoise

Turtleneck under sweatshirt, but with jewelry

T-shirts tied at one side

White T-shirt hanging beneath sweatshirt

Preppy Subset:

Anything pink and green

Argyle socks

Argyle sweater vests

Corduroy shorts

Headbands

Izods

Penny loafers or Top-siders

Plaid

Polos

Sweater wrapped around shoulders and knotted in front

The Most Fashionable Dudes Had to Be Seen In...

Bomber jackets

British Knights shoes

Camouflage clothing, even on small children

Chuck Taylor shoes (mixing up the colors)

Collars up

Converse tennis shoes

Do-rags

Duck shoes

Eastlands

"Frankie Says" T-shirts

Hawaiian look

High tops

Izod

Jean jackets

Lumber jack vests

Mirrored sunglasses

Mismatched socks

Mohawks

Nikes

Ocean Pacific

One earring (left ear)

Oxford shirts

Panama Jack hats

Parachute pants

Pastel linen blazers

Pockets, pockets everywhere

Polos

Ponytails

Rattails

Ray Bans

Sexy stubble, if facial hair was available, á la George Michael

Shapes shaved into hair with razor

Suspenders (rainbow or Michael J. Fox version)

Sweats

Ties: thin, knit, or sock

Top-siders—boat shoes

T-shirts ripped, hanging off shoulder

Vans

Zipper jackets á la Michael Jackson

These Were Our Secrets to Beautiful—and Big—Hair

Aqua Net
Aussie hair products
Banana clips
Bangs that looked like tsunamis!
Berets
Bilevel hair
Colorful foam rollers that were bent and slept in
Crimping irons
Dep
Dippity-Do
Dorothy Hammill haircuts or pixie cuts
Floppy, mesh hair bows
Gel
Glittery hair, makeup, and fingernails
Hairspray
Headbands (terry cloth)
Jhirmack

L.A. Looks
Mousse
Nexxus
Permed bobs
Pert
Picks
Ponytails on the side
Prell
Rave
Redken
Ribboned hair barettes
Salon Selectives
Scrunchies
Spiral perms
Spritz
Stiff Stuff
Suave
Sun In
Vidal Sassoon
Wet look
Wet 'N Wild
Wingy, feathery hair on the sides
Z-combs

It Wasn't As Simple as Throwing on a Pair of Jeans:

Jean Designers and Looks

DESIGNERS:

Calvin Klein, Chic, Gloria Vanderbilt, Guess?,
Jordache, Lee, Levi's, Sasson, Sergio Valente,
Wrangler

LOOKS:

Acid-washed
Bandana tied around leg
Designer
Jean shorts from *Dirty Dancing,* cut-off and cuffed
Patches on the butt
Ripped knees
Safety pins on jeans
Socks outside
Tight (very)
Tiny ankles or peg-legging
Zippers at ankles

We Were Living in a Material World and She Was the Material Girl:

Madonna Styles We Emulated

Bare navel ✳ Biker shorts ✳ Black clothing

Bleached short hair ✳ Boy-Toy belt buckles

Bras outside clothing and generally

exposed under net shirts ✳ Crosses

Exposed dark roots ✳ Fingerless lace gloves

Fishnet stockings

Flared slip skirts with tennis shoes

Floppy net bow as headband

Hair pulled with net bow ✱ *Heavy eye makeup*

Jean jacket ✱ *Leather/lace together*

Leggings under short skirts ✱ *Little boots*

Loose/fly-away hair ✱ *Marilyn Monroe retro*

(as in "Material Girl" video)

Mole near lips ✱ *Mucho bracelets*

Shoe brands—
Some of Which Have Endured

Adidas
British Knights
Candies
Capezio
Cherokee
Chuck Taylor
Converse
Eastlands
Etonic
Jellies
Kangaroos
Keds
L.A. Gear
Nike (including "Cortez" cross-trainers)
Nine West
Pony
Puma
Reebok
Saucony
Sporto duck boots
Vans

The Essential Scents for
Love in the '80s

Anais Anais	Lauren
Beautiful	Love's Baby Soft
Benetton	Obsession
Brut	Old Spice
Diva	Polo
Drakkar	Royal Copenhagen
Electric Youth	Scaasi
Engele	Stetson
Giorgio	Tabu
Gloria Vanderbilt	Verve
Halston	White Linen
High Karate	White Shoulders

Gee, Aren't These Beauty Products Terrific!

Aime

Blue eyeshadow and mascara

Bonne Bell

Clearasil

Glitter for body/face

Lee Press On Nails

L'Erin

Lip gloss

Lip Smacker

Liquid eyeliners

Love's Baby Soft

Max Factor

Merle Norman

Mood lipsticks

Noxema

Pearl Drops

Sea Breeze

Stridex

Ten-O-Six

worldly events, hot beds of activity, disasters, and oh, the embarrassments and scandals . . .

THE WORLD/NEWS of the '80s

THE WORLD/
NEWS

AIRMAIL

Events in the World:
Beginnings and Endings

Acid use increases

Aid: Live, Band, Farm

AIDS

Anorexia and bulimia reach new heights

ATMs proliferate

Baby Fae receives baboon heart

Baby M case

Barney Clark gets the first permanent artificial heart transplant

Bell phone breaks up

Berlin Wall crumbles, and with it communism from Berlin to Romania

Bryant Gumbel starts his run on the *Today* show

***Cats* opens**

Central Park jogger is beaten and raped

CNN

"Condom," the word, is first used on network TV

Elizabeth Jordan Carr is the United States' first test-tube baby

Elizabeth Kane is the United States' first surrogate mother

Duran Duran takes a hiatus

Greedy yuppies charge themselves into debt

Greg LeMond is the first American to win the Tour de France

Halley's Comet arrives

Hands Across America

Highly addictive crack use reaches epidemic proportions

Home Shopping Network opens for business

John Belushi overdoses and dies

John Lennon is shot

L'esperance family gives birth to in-vitro quintuplets

Low-cal foods obsession hits the nation

Lyme disease breakout

Manuel Noriega is flushed out of Panama

Mary Lou Retton is the first woman to appear on a Wheaties box

M*A*S*H goes off the air

Meese Report links sex and violence

Michael Jackson begins *Thriller* tour in Kansas City

MTV is born

NutraSweet debuts

Oprah starts her show

Pizza delivery becomes mainstream

Political correctness

Pop-tops on cans are phased out

Post-it Notes

Reaganomics and the Trickle-Down Theory of Economics

Recycling kick

Robert Bork is nixed as appointee to Supreme Court

Ronald Reagan gets shot

Rush Limbaugh begins a syndicated talk-radio program

Safety seals on all containers become mandatory after cyanide found in Tylenol capsules

Sally Ride is first woman in space

Samantha Smith travels to the Soviet Union at Yuri Andropov's invitation

Sanctions against South Africa to protest apartheid

Sandra Day O'Connor is first woman appointed to the Supreme Court

South American rain forests are stripped at an alarming rate

Space shuttle is launched for first time

Star Wars defense system unveiled

Statue of Liberty gets a face-lift

Styrofoam dominates for fast food containers

The term "Yuppies" is born

***Titanic* wreckage is located**

USA Today goes to press

Van Halen breaks up

Vietnam War Memorial unveiled

***Voyager I* photographs Saturn's rings**

Walter Cronkite retires

Hot Beds of Activity that Frequently Appeared on the Evening News

Afghanistan
China
Colombia
East Germany
Egypt
Falkland Islands
Grenada
Haiti
Honduras
Iran
Iraq
Ireland
Israel
Lebanon
Libya
Nicaragua
North and South Korea
Panama
Philippines
South Africa
The Soviet Union

Disasters:
Both Natural and Man-made

- Acid rain
- Air disasters:

    Korean Airlines Flight 007 is "accidentally" shot down by Soviet Defense System; 206 are killed

    Mideast-related terrorists blow up Pan Am Flight 103 over Lockerbie, Scotland, killing 259 aboard and eleven villagers

    Air Florida flight crashes into icy Potomac River, killing 82

    Pan Am Flight 159 crashes in New Orleans, killing 154

    Delta Air Lines crash at Dallas-Fort Worth Airport kills 133

- Black Monday

- Blizzard on Mt. Hood in Oregon kills several hikers

- Blizzard stretching from Maine to Florida causes thirty-seven deaths

- Challenger explosion

- Chernobyl's reactor meltdown in the Soviet Union

- Crowded skywalk in Kansas City Hyatt Regency hotel collapses, killing 114

- Cyanide-laced Tylenol caplets

- Exxon *Valdez* spill in Alaska's Prince William Sound

- Flooding in California, Arizona, and Mexico kills thirty-six

- Freighter named *Summit Venture* collides with bridge in Tampa, Florida; thirty-five are killed

- Hurricane Gloria

- Jessica McClure is trapped in well in Texas for fifty-eight hours

- Love Canal in New York is declared a disaster area due to toxic waste contamination

- Mt. Saint Helen's eruption kills fifty-seven

- Ozone problems reach new heights with discovery of hole

- Race riots in Florida result in fourteen deaths and three hundred injuries

- Starvation in Ethiopia saddens world and leads to USA for Africa group

- Turret #2 on battleship *Iowa* explodes, killing forty-seven

- Union Carbide chemical gas leak in Bhopal, India, kills 1,700

- U.S. Marines killed in their Beirut barracks

- USS *Vincennes* opens fire on an Iranian passenger jet in the Persian Gulf; 290 aboard Iran Air are killed

- Volcanic eruptions in Alaska

- World Series earthquake in San Francisco

'80s EMBARRASSMENTS

Beta

Broken nose fiasco on *Geraldo*

"The Butt" (a dance)

Captain Midnight, a video terrorist, jams HBO broadcast for 30 seconds

Chief medical examiner for the state of Connecticut is terminated for bringing her dogs into autopsies with her

Chinese pandas at the National Zoo refuse to mate

DeLoreans

Diana Spencer, future Princess of Wales, is photographed without a slip

English and Italian soccer fans riot in Brussels, killing thirty-eight

Failed rescue of U.S. hostages in Iran. Eight commandos are killed.

Former National Security Agency employee found guilty of secretly spying for KGB at U.S. embassy in Moscow

Garbage barge from New York carrying 3,100 tons of trash floats aimlessly without a place to unload

Genital herpes is a frequent source of amusement on
Saturday Night Live

Geraldo Rivera's "discoveries" in Al Capone's vault

Homelessness receives national attention

Interior Secretary James Watt halted new endangered species
listings for thirteen months

Matthias Rust, a West German teenager, flies a single engine
plane into Red Square in Moscow

Milli Vanilli

Morton Downey Jr. blames swastikas on face on skinheads

New Coke

Oprah Winfrey's not-so-permanent weight loss

The Reagan kids (book and *SNL* appearance)

Rejection of Ryan White, a child with AIDS, by school
and community

Tiananmen Square massacre

Washington Post caves under pressure from CIA to edit
a Bob Woodward article

White beluga whale is mysteriously killed off Long Island Sound

White guys dressing up like Michael Jackson
and thinking they were cool

Got Enough Shoes, Imelda?:
'80s Scandals

Bounty placed on Salman Rushdie's head for writing *Satanic Verses*

Claus von Bulow on trial for attempted murder of wife Sunny (she's still in a coma to this day)

Dan Rather is beaten while strolling on Park Avenue late at night ("What's the frequency, Kenneth?")

Elizabeth Morgan serves jail time for contempt of court in a custody battle for not revealing the location of her daughter

Eugene Hasenfus, a pilot, is shot down in Nicaragua, and Iran-Contra unravels

Fawn Hall and late-night shredding

Gary Hart's monkey business with Donna Rice ends his presidential run

John Gotti is acquitted

Imelda Marcos' extensive shoe collection

Jim Bakker's monkey business with Jessica Hahn

Jimmy Swaggart visits prostitutes in New Orleans

Mayflower Madam Sidney Biddle Barrows is arrested

Milli Vanilli charade

Miss America nude photo scandal with Vanessa Williams

Nancy Reagan consults with astrologer

Nancy Reagan dances with Frank Sinatra

Oral Roberts raises money to get the price off his head that he says God has placed there

Pete Rose gambles on baseball and is banned from baseball for life

Pope John Paul II is shot in St. Peter's Square by Turkish radical

Prince Charles' continuing affair with Camilla Parker

Princess Diana's affair with James Gilbey

Retarded teenage girl is sexually molested by high school athletes in New Jersey

Rob Lowe videos himself having sex with a minor

Rock Hudson exposes his lover to AIDS

Savings and loans scandals

Silicone breast implants found to be dangerous

Tiananmen Square: 300 student demonstrators are killed

Traci Lords admits she was fifteen when she first began pornography

U.S.A. boycotts the Moscow Olympics in 1980; the Soviet Union returns the favor in 1984, boycotting the Los Angeles games

Woody Allen prepares to rob the cradle

Wrongful imprisonment results in eventual release of Gerry Conlon (England)

leavin' behind the '70s, new technologies or products, cars, looking forward . . .

TECHNOLOGY of the '80s

TECHNOLOGY

It Was, Fer Shurrr, a Relief to Leave These '70s Things Behind as We Ushered in the '80s

'70s '70s '70s

Afros with picks sticking out

Airbrush murals on vans and cars

Big collars

Black-and-white TVs

Confusing times of dropouts, protesters, and social unrest

Disco

Eight-track tapes

ERA battles

Evel Knievel stunts

False eyelashes

Farrah Fawcett wigs

Floppy bell bottoms

Frosted blue eye shadow

Gas shortages and lines at the pump

Goatees

Hard-to-park, gas-guzzling boat cars

**Hooking your computer up to your TV
because you had no other options**

Hostage crisis in Iran

Jimmy Carter

Leisure suits

Long, hard-to-wash hair

LSD

'70s '70s '70

Mass quantities of polyester

Neck-breaking platform shoes

Nixon

Oil embargoes

Pintos that exploded on rear impact

Pull-top cans

Roller boogie

Station wagons

Streaking

Swinging and swapping parties

Terrorism at home

TVs with only thirteen channels

The Village People

Vinyl record albums that skipped if you breathed on them

Your-fault divorce

Totally Radical
New Technologies or Products:

Air bags

Amiga computers

Answering machines

Apple computers

Atari 2600

Bras on sports cars and Jeeps

Boom boxes

Cable TV

Call waiting

CD players

Channel surfing

Coleco

Combination phone and answering machines

Commodore 64 computers

Cordless phones

Direct TV

Faxing

FedEx (Federal Express then)

Futons

Game Boy

Heart rate and blood pressure machines in Wal-Marts

Intellevision

Laser disc videos

Lycra begins finding its way into more clothing
(and everyone can breathe a little easier)

Microwave meals

Microwaves everywhere (home, QuikTrip, work)

Minivans

Mountain bikes

Pizza delivery MTV

Post-its

Satellite dishes Sporks

TI 994A (tape deck computer)

Tinted glass on car windows

Universal remote controls

VCRs—VHS or Beta? *Walkmans*

Word processors

I've Got Me a Chrysler, It's as Big as a Whale:

Cruisin' Machines

Beretta	🚓	Chevy Corvette
BMW	🚓	Chevy Z28
Camaro	🚓	Camaro IROC-Z28
DeLorean	🚓	Dodge Spirit
Chevy Caprice	🚓	Ford Escort

Ford Fiesta	🚓	Mustang convertibles
Ford Probe	🚓	Nissan 280ZX
Ford Taurus	🚓	Nissan 300 ZX
Ford Tempo	🚓	Pontiac Fiero
Gremlin	🚓	Saab
Honda Civic	🚓	Suzuki Samurai
Honda CRX	🚓	Trans AM
Horizon	🚓	Volkswagen Rabbit
K-Car	🚓	Yugo GV
Maserati	🚓	Yugo GVL
Mazda RX-7	🚓	Yugo GVX
Mercedes	🚓	

Things We Had to Look Forward To ...

An all-CD music collection

AOL

Beepers

Busy signals due to people on-line

Caller ID, call blocker

Cell phones

Stephen Covey seminars

Drive-through pharmacies

Electronic planners or Palm Pilots
(even Franklin Day Planners were rare)

E-mail

Expanded ZIP Code numbers

Food delivery on a grand scale

Grunge

Internet surfing

Internet banking

Modems

Numerous numbers to remember:
home, work, fax, beeper, cell phone, E-mail

Personal computers in homes

PG-13 ratings

Portable CD players

Prepackaged food on a grand scale

Superstores and chains taking over
the marketplace

SUVs sweeping suburbia

Thirty-three-cent stamps

Tons of passwords to keep track of

Video stores on every corner

the biggest shows, actresses, actors, emmy winners, made-for-TV shows, game shows, Saturday Night Live characters, memorable quotes, inseparable buds . . .

TELEVISION of the '80s

TELEVISION

AIR MAIL

The Television Shows of the Decade

Barbara Mandrell and the Mandrell Sisters
Battlestar Galactica
Benson
B.J. and the Bear
Blue Thunder
The Bold and the Beautiful
Bosom Buddies
Buck Rogers in the 25th Century

The A-Team
ABC After-School Specials
Alf
Alice
All My Children
America's Most Wanted
Another World

Cagney & Lacey
Charles in Charge
Charlie's Angels
Cheers
Comic Relief
The Cosby Show
Cosmos
Dallas

Dynasty
Falcon Crest
The Fall Guy
Fame
Family Ties
Fantasy Island
Friday Night Videos
General Hospital
Gimme a Break

The Golden Girls
The Greatest
*   American Hero*
Growing Pains
Guiding Light
Hart to Hart
Head of the Class
Hill Street Blues

177
TELEVISION

Hunter
The Incredible Hulk
The Jeffersons
Kate & Allie
Knots Landing
L.A. Law
Late Night with
    David Letterman

Moonlighting
Mork & Mindy
MTV Headbanger's Ball
Murder, She Wrote
Murphy Brown
My Sister Sam
Newhart
Night Court

Life Goes On
Lifestyles of the Rich
    and Famous
The Love Boat
Love Connection
MacGyver
Magnum P.I.
M*A*S*H*
Miami Vice

POSTCARDS FROM THE '80S

Nightline
Night Tracks
One Day at a Time
Our House
Perfect Strangers
Punky Brewster
Puttin' on the Hits
Quantum Leap

Simon & Simon
60 Minutes
Solid Gold
Square Pegs
Star Search
Three's Company
Too Close for Comfort
21 Jump Street

Quincy, M. E.
Riptide
Roseanne
St. Elsewhere
Santa Barbara
Saturday Night Live
Scarecrow and Mrs. King
Silver Spoons

20/20
Voyagers
Webster
Who's the Boss?
WKRP in Cincinnati
The Wonder Years
Yo! MTV Raps
The Young and the Restless

TV Actresses Who Scream '80s

Kirstie Alley
Catherine Bach
Justine Bateman
Meredith Baxter-Birney
Mayim Bialik
Lisa Bonet
Nell Carter
Mindy Cohn
Joan Collins
Tyne Daly
Pam Dawber
Linda Evans
Kim Fields

Melissa Gilbert

Sharon Gless

Linda Gray

Veronica Hamel

Katherine Helmond

Polly Holliday

Kate Jackson

Linda Lavin

Judith Light

Heather Locklear

Shelley Long

Pamela Sue Martin

Nancy McKeon

Alyssa Milano

Donna Mills

Sarah Jessica Parker

Rhea Perlman

Stefanie Powers

Priscilla Presley

Victoria Principal

Charlotte Rae

Meg Ryan

Cybill Shepherd

Jaclyn Smith

Heather Thomas

Charlene Tilton

Tracey Ullman

Joan Van Ark

Lisa Whelchel

Tina Yothers

Stephanie Zimbalist

181
TELEVISION

TV Actors Who Bellow '80s

Alan Alda
Harry Anderson
Richard Dean
   Anderson
Dan Aykroyd
Scott Baio
Jason Bateman
Jim Belushi
Bill Bixby
Bruce Boxleitner
Pierce Brosnan
Kirk Cameron
Dabney Coleman
Gary Coleman
Bill Cosby
Ted Danson
Tony Danza
Patrick Duffy

Greg Evigan
Lou Ferrigno
John Forsythe
Michael J. Fox
Kelsey Grammer
Richard Grieco
Larry Hagman
Tom Hanks
Kadeem Hardison
Mark Harmon
David Hasselhoff
Howard Hesseman
Don Johnson
Joey Lawrence
John Larroquette
Emmanuel Lewis
Lee Majors
Ricardo Montalban
Mr. T
Ron Perlman
Joe Piscopo
John Ratzenberger

Paul Reiser
Alfonzo Ribiero
John Ritter
Fred Savage
John Schneider
Ricky Schroder
Tom Selleck
Martin Short
Rick Springfield
Vic Tayback
Alan Thicke
Daniel J. Travanti
John Travolta
Scott Valentine
Robert Wagner
Malcolm Jamal
  Warner
George Wendt
Robin Williams
Bruce Willis
Tom Wopat

The Emmys in the '80s

1980

Outstanding Drama Series.....*Hill Street Blues*
Outstanding Comedy Series.....*Taxi*

1981

Outstanding Drama Series.....*Hill Street Blues*
Outstanding Comedy Series.....*Barney Miller*

1982

Outstanding Drama Series.....*Hill Street Blues*
Outstanding Comedy Series.....*Cheers*

1983

Outstanding Drama Series.....*Hill Street Blues*
Outstanding Comedy Series.....*Cheers*

1984

Outstanding Drama Series.....*Cagney and Lacey*
Outstanding Comedy Series.....*The Cosby Show*

1985

Outstanding Drama Series.....*Cagney and Lacey*
Outstanding Comedy Series.....*The Golden Girls*

1986

Outstanding Drama Series.....*L.A. Law*
Outstanding Comedy Series.....*The Golden Girls*

1987

Outstanding Drama Series.....*thirtysomething*
Outstanding Comedy Series.....*The Wonder Years*

1988

Outstanding Drama Series.....*L.A. Law*
Outstanding Comedy Series.....*Cheers*

1989

Outstanding Drama Series.....*L.A. Law*
Outstanding Comedy Series.....*Murphy Brown*

A Unique Art Form:
Made-for-TV or "The Story of" Movies

Adam • *Alien Nation* • *The Ann Jillian Story* • *The Best Little Girl in the World* • *Betrayed by Innocence* • *Beverly Hills Madam* • *Blood Money: The Story of Clinton and Nadine* • *Blood Vows: The Story of a Mafia Wife* • *The Blue and the Gray* • *The Burning Bed* • *A Case of Deadly Force* • *The Case of the Hillside*

Stranglers • Christopher Columbus • The Chronicles of Narnia • Cocaine: One Man's Seduction • The Day After • A Day for Thanks on Waltons' Mountain • The Deliberate Stranger • Don't Look Back: The Story of Leroy "Satchel" Paige • Elvis and Me • The Ewok Adventure • Ewoks: The Battle for Endor • Finnegan Begin Again • George Washington • Grace Kelly • Guyana Tragedy: The Story of Jim Jones • Hands of a Stranger • The Hearst and Davies Affair • Jacqueline Bouvier

Kennedy • **The Jesse Owens Story** • *John and Yoko: A Love Story* • Kenny Rogers as the Gambler (Parts 1–3) • *Lonesome Dove* • **Mafia Princess** • Madonna: Innocence Lost • Marilyn: The Untold Story • *M*A*S*H: Goodbye, Farewell and Amen* • Mayflower Madam • **Miami Vice** and **Miami Vice 2: The Prodigal Son** • *North and South* and *North and South II* • Policewoman Centerfold • Poor Little Rich Girl: The Barbara Hutton Story •

The Preppie Murder • Quarterback Princess • Return to Mayberry • The Revenge of Al Capone • Revenge of the Stepford Wives • Roe vs. Wade • Roots: The Gift • Shogun • Small Sacrifices • The Taking of Flight 847: The Uli Derickson Story • The Thorn Birds • Unnatural Causes • V • A Very Brady Christmas • The Waltons: The Christmas Carol • War and Remembrance • Windmills of the Gods • The Winds of War

Our Next Contestant Is:
TV Game Shows

Card Sharks

Hollywood Squares

Jeopardy!

The Joker's Wild

Love Connection

The New Dating Game

Press Your Luck ("No Whammies!")

The Price Is Right

Remote Control

Tic Tac Dough

The $20,000 Pyramid, The $25,000 Pyramid,
and The $50,000 Pyramid

Wheel of Fortune

Yeah, That's the Ticket!: *SNL* Players of the '80s and Their Memorable Characters

Jim Belushi 1983–85
Santa, the Terminator • Rosemary Clooney • Jennifer Beals

Dana Carvey 1986–93
Garth Algar • George Bush • The Church Lady • Hans • Johnny Carson • Massive Headwound Harry • Jimmy Stewart • George Michael

Billy Crystal 1984–85
Fernando • Sammy Davis, Jr. • Frankie (The "Don't You Hate It When . . . " Guy) • Muhammad Ali • Howard Cosell

Joan Cusak 1985–86
Brooke Shields • Jane Fonda

Robin Duke 1981–84
Wendy Whiner • Shari Lewis (with Lambchop) • Eva Braun

Nora Dunn 1985–90
Leona Helmsley • Pat Stevens • Babette ("Weekend Update" correspondent) • Wayne Campbell's mom

Al Franken 1979–80, 1988–95

Stuart Smalley • Pat Robertson • Jim Bakker • "Weekend Update" mobile reporter

Mary Gross 1981–85

"Weekend Update" anchor • Alfalfa • Mary Tyler Moore • Dr. Ruth Westheimer

Christopher Guest 1984–85

"Weekend Update" anchor • Nigel Tufnel • Synchronized swimming coach

Brad Hall 1982–84

John Hinkley • El Dorko's friend Mike • The Human Stapler • John Delorean • Walter Mondale

Phil Hartman 1986–94

Bill Clinton • Barbara Bush • Frankenstein • Unfrozen Caveman Lawyer • Burt Reynolds

Jan Hooks 1986–91

Hillary Clinton • Sinead O'Connor • Nancy Reagan • Tammy Faye Bakker • Sally Jesse Raphael

Victoria Jackson 1986–92

Roseanne Arnold • Cyndi Lauper • Cindy Brady • Toonces's owner • Tipper Gore

Julia Louis-Dreyfus 1982–85

Rhoda • Diana Ross • Marie Osmond

Jon Lovitz 1985–90

Master Thespian • Tonto • Satan • Annoying Man • Manuel Noriega • The Pathological Liar

Dennis Miller 1985–91

"Weekend Update" anchor • Gary Hart • George Harrison

Eddie Murphy 1980–84

Buh-Weet • Gumby • Mr. Robinson • Stevie Wonder • Mr. T

Mike Myers 1988–95

Wayne Campbell • Simon • Mick Jagger • Barbra Streisand • Jewish mother

Kevin Nealon 1987–95

"Weekend Update" anchor • Sam Donaldson • Mr. Subliminal • Tarzan • Franz

Joe Piscopo 1980–84

Frank Sinatra • Doug Whiner • Ted Koppel • Phil Donahue • Sports guy for "Weekend Update"

Randy Quaid 1985–86

Ronald Reagan • Vlad the Impaler • Ed McMahon

Martin Short 1984–85

Ed Grimley • Katharine Hepburn • Nathan Thurm, the nervous lawyer • Synchronized swimmer • Paul Simon

"I can't believe my grandmother just felt me up!":

Memorable Quotes
from Movies and Television

*". . . and my name is Charlie.
They work for me."*
Charlie's Angels

"As you wish."
The Princess Bride

*"Children, can you say,
'scumbucket'?"*
"Mr. Robinson's Neighborhood," *SNL*

*"Could you describe the
ruckus, sir?"*
The Breakfast Club

"De plane! De plane!"
Fantasy Island

"Do you want to pet my monkey?"
"Sprockets," *SNL*

"E.T. phone home."
E.T.: The Extra-Terrestrial

"Freeze gopher!"
Caddyshack

"I can't believe my grandmother just felt me up!"
Sixteen Candles

"I gave her my heart. She gave me a pen."
Say Anything

"I'm a kid; that's my job."
Uncle Buck

"I'm a single, successful guy."
Fast Times at Ridgemont High

"I pity the fool!"
Mr. T

"It's a Cinderella story."
Caddyshack

"It's better to look good than to feel good, and darling, you look marvelous!"
"Fernando," *SNL*

"Jane, you ignorant slut."
"Weekend Update," *SNL*

"Life moves pretty fast. If you don't stop and look around for a while, you could miss it."
Ferris Bueller's Day Off

"Married, yes married."
Sixteen Candles

"Minor flesh wound"
Monty Python, The Search for the Holy Grail

"Nerds! Nerds!"
Revenge of the Nerds

"Norm!"
Cheers

"No. There is another."
The Empire Strikes Back

"Nothin' but the best."
National Lampoon's Vacation

"Save Ferris!"
Ferris Bueller's Day Off

"Score. Direct hit."
Sixteen Candles

"Sometimes ya just gotta say, 'What the f---.'"
Risky Business

"Those aren't pillows!"
Planes, Trains & Automobiles

"Wax on. Wax off."
Karate Kid

"We are the knights who say 'Nee.'"
Monty Python, The Search for the Holy Grail

"We're on a mission from God."
The Blues Brothers

"What you talkin' 'bout, Willis?"
Diff'rent Strokes

"When you tell a story, have a point!"
Planes, Trains & Automobiles

"Wonder Twin powers activate!"
The Super Friends

"You must chill!"
Say Anything

"You wanna go where everybody knows your name."
Cheers

We're on a Mission from God:
Whether by Circumstance or True Fondness,
Inseparable Buds from Film and Television

Al and Birdy ■ *Birdy*

The A-Team

Balki and Larry ■ *Perfect Strangers*

Bill and Ted ■ *Bill and Ted's Excellent Adventure*

B.J. and the Bear

Bo and Luke Duke ■ *The Dukes of Hazzard*

Bob and Doug McKenzie ■ *Strange Brew*

Christine Cagney and Mary Beth Lacey ■ *Cagney & Lacey*

Cates and Reggie ■ *48 HRS.*

Celie and Shug Avery ■ *The Color Purple*

Cheech and Chong

Crash Davis and "Nuke" Laloosh ■ *Bull Durham*

Sonny Crockett and Ricardo Tubbs ■ *Miami Vice*

Daisy and Hoke ■ *Driving Miss Daisy*

Daisy, Kat, and Jojo ■ *Mystic Pizza*

Daniel and Miyagi ■ *Karate Kid*

Danny and Ray ■ *Running Scared*

Daulton Lee and Christopher Boyce ■ *The Falcon and the Snowman*

David Addison and Maddie Hayes ■ *Moonlighting*

Dee Dee McCall and Rick Hunter ■ *Hunter*

Del Griffith and Neal Page ■ *Planes, Trains & Automobiles*

E.T. and Elliot ■ *E.T.: The Extra-Terrestrial*

Frankie and Joey ■ *SNL*

The Golden Girls

Hanz and Franz ■ *SNL*

Jack Walsh and Jonathan Mardukas ■ *Midnight Run*

Jake and Elwood ■ *The Blues Brothers*

Joanie and Chachi ■ *Happy Days* and
Joanie Loves Chachi

Kate & Allie

203
TELEVISION

Kip/Buffy and Henry/Hildegarde ■ *Bosom Buddies*

Larry, Darryl, and Darryl ■ *Newhart*

Lewis, Gilbert, Wormser, Booger, Lamar, Poindexter ■
Revenge of the Nerds

Lieutenant Speer and Mike Murphy ■ *City Heat*

Thomas Magnum and Jonathan Higgins ■ *Magnum, P.I.*

Maverick and Goose ■ *Top Gun*

Michael and Elliot ■ *thirtysomething*

Michael Knight and KITT ■ *Knight Rider*

Mikey, Brand, Chunk, Mouth, Andy, Stef ■ *The Goonies*

Milo and Otis ■ *The Adventures of Milo and Otis*

Paul Pfeiffer and Kevin Arnold ■ *The Wonder Years*

Riggs and Murtaugh ■ *Lethal Weapon*

Roberta and Susan ■ *Desperately Seeking Susan*

Roger and Eddie Valiant ■ *Who Framed Roger Rabbit?*

Sam, Sarah, Nick, Michael, Chloe, Harold, Meg, Karen ■
The Big Chill

"Scarecrow" and Amanda King ■
Scarecrow and Mrs. King

A.J. Simon and Rick Simon ■ *Simon & Simon*

Scott Turner and Hooch ■ *Turner & Hooch*

Zan and Jayna ■ *The Wonder Twins*

classic movies, actresses, actors—both good and bad, golden globe winners, oscar winners, top-grossing flicks, slasher films, sequels, sequels, and more sequels . . .

FILM of the '80s

FILM

'Classic '80s Movie Fare

About Last Night . . .

Adventures in Babysitting

Against All Odds

Aliens

Airplane!

Amadeus

An American Werewolf in London

Bachelor Party

Batman

Back to the Future

Beetlejuice

Better Off Dead

Beverly Hills Cop

The Big Chill

The Big Easy

Blade Runner

Blind Date

The Blues Brothers

The Breakfast Club

Bright Lights, Big City

Caddyshack

Cannonball Run

Can't Buy Me Love

Chariots of Fire

Clue

Cocktail

Cocoon

The Color of Money

The Color Purple

Crocodile Dundee

Dead Poets Society

Die Hard

Driving Miss Daisy

The Elephant Man

The Empire Strikes Back

E.T.: The Extra-Terrestrial

Explorers

Fame

Fast Times at Ridgemont High

Fatal Attraction

Ferris Bueller's Day Off

Field of Dreams

A Fish Called Wanda

Flashdance

Fletch

Footloose

Full Metal Jacket

Gandhi

Ghostbusters

Girls Just Want to Have Fun

Gleaming the Cube

The Goonies

Grease 2

The Great Outdoors

Gremlins

Halloween 2

Hard to Hold

The History of the World: Part I

Howard the Duck

The Howling

Indiana Jones Trilogy: *Raiders of the Lost Ark,
The Temple of Doom, The Last Crusade*

Jewel of the Nile

The Karate Kid

The Last Emperor

Lethal Weapon

The Little Mermaid

Mad Max series

The Lost Boys

Mask

Meatballs 2

Monty Python's The Meaning of Life

Moonstruck

Mr. Mom

My Chauffer

National Lampoon's Vacation

The Natural

A Nightmare on Elm Street series

9 1/2 Weeks

9 to 5

An Officer and a Gentleman

One Crazy Summer

On Golden Pond

Out of Africa

The Outsiders

Pee Wee's Big Adventure

213
FILM

Platoon

Police Academy

Porky's

Predator

Private Benjamin

Purple Rain

Raging Bull

Rain Man

Raising Arizona

Red Dawn

Real Genius

The Return of the Jedi

Revenge of the Nerds

Risky Business

RoboCop

Rocky II, III, and IV

Romancing the Stone

A Room with a View

St. Elmo's Fire

Say Anything

Scarface

Sea of Love

Seventh Sign

sex, lies and videotape

Short Circuit

Silverado

Sixteen Candles

Solarbabies

Some Kind of Wonderful

Splash

Spaceballs

Star Trek: The Motion Picture

Staying Alive

Streets of Fire

Stripes

The Sure Thing

This Is Spinal Tap

Three Amigos

Tootsie

Top Gun

Top Secret!

Trading Places

Tremors

Two of a Kind

Under the Cherry Moon

The Untouchables

Valley Girl

War Games

Weird Science

The Witches of Eastwick

The World According to Garp

Xanadu

Youngblood

Young Guns

Zapped!

So-Fine
Actresses from the Big Screen

Ellen Barkin
Drew Barrymore
Kim Basinger
Phoebe Cates
Glenn Close
Joan Cusack
Geena Davis
Bo Derek
Carrie Fisher
Jodie Foster
Teri Garr
Whoopi Goldberg
Holly Hunter
Jennifer Jason Leigh
Andie MacDowell
Mary Stuart Masterson
Marlee Matlin
Edie McClurg
Kelly McGillis

Demi Moore
Mary-Louise Parker
Dolly Parton
Molly Ringwald
Julia Roberts
Meg Ryan
Winona Ryder
Susan Sarandon
Ally Sheedy
Brooke Shields
Elisabeth Shue
Ione Skye
Helen Slater
Sissy Spacek
Meryl Streep
Barbra Streisand
Jessica Tandy
Lea Thompson
Lily Tomlin
Kathleen Turner
Sigourney Weaver
Debra Winger
Daphne Zuniga

219 FILM

So-Fine
Actors from the Big Screen

Kevin Bacon	Michael Douglas
Warren Beatty	Robert Downy Jr.
James Belushi	Clint Eastwood
Matthew Broderick	Anthony Edwards
Nicolas Cage	Emilio Estevez
John Candy	Corey Feldman
Chevy Chase	Harrison Ford
Thomas Chong	Richard Gere
Kevin Costner	Mel Gibson
Tom Cruise	Danny Glover
Jon Cryer	Steve Guttenberg
Billy Crystal	Corey Haim
John Cusack	Anthony Michael Hall
Johnny Depp	Mark Hamil
Matt Dillon	Tom Hanks
Kirk Douglas	Hulk Hogan

C. Thomas Howell
Michael Keaton
Val Kilmer
Rob Lowe
Ralph Macchio
Cheech Marin
Steve Martin
Andrew McCarthy
Dudley Moore
Eddie Murphy
Bill Murray
Judd Nelson
Paul Newman
Jack Nicholson
Leslie Nielsen
Nick Nolte
Sean Penn

River Phoenix
Robert Redford
Christopher Reeve
Judge Reinhold
Burt Reynolds
Mickey Rourke
Kurt Russell
Arnold Schwarzenegger
Charlie Sheen
James Spader
Slyvester Stallone
Eric Stoltz
Kiefer Sutherland
Patrick Swayze
Robin Williams
Bruce Willis

Gag Me with a Spoon:
The Worst Actors and Actresses of the Decade

Kirstie Alley
Catherine Bach
Scott Baio
Jason Bateman
Justine Bateman
Meredith Baxter-Birney
Kirk Cameron
Cheech and Chong
Kevin Costner
Tony Danza
Bo Derek
Emilio Estevez
Corey Feldman
Lou Ferrigno

Steve Guttenberg
David Hasselhoff
C. Thomas Howell
Don Johnson
Joey Lawrence
Shelley Long
Rob Lowe
Andie MacDowell
Andrew McCarthy
Kelly McGillis
Demi Moore
Mr. T
Julia Roberts
John Schneider
Ricky Schroder
Arnold Schwarzenegger
Cybill Shepherd
Sylvester Stallone
Patrick Swayze
Tom Wopat
Tina Yothers

223 FILM

Golden Globe Winners

1980
Drama: *Kramer vs. Kramer*
Musical/Comedy: *Breaking Away*

1981
Drama: *Ordinary People*
Musical/Comedy: *Coal Miner's Daughter*

1982
Drama: *On Golden Pond*
Musical/Comedy: *Arthur*

1983
Drama: *E.T.: The Extra-Terrestrial*
Musical/Comedy: *Tootsie*

1984
Drama: *Terms of Endearment*
Musical/Comedy: *Yentl*

1985
Drama: *Amadeus*
Musical/Comedy: *Romancing the Stone*

1986
Drama: *Out of Africa*
Musical/Comedy: *Prizzi's Honor*

1987
Drama: *Platoon*
Musical/Comedy: *Hannah and Her Sisters*

1988
Drama: *The Last Emperor*
Musical/Comedy: *Hope and Glory*

1989
Drama: *Rain Man*
Musical/Comedy: *Working Girl*

OSCAR
Winners

19**80**

Best Picture *Ordinary People*
Best Actor Robert De Niro in *Raging Bull*
Best Actress Sissy Spacek in *Coal Miner's Daughter*

19**81**

Best Picture *Chariots of Fire*
Best Actor Henry Fonda in *On Golden Pond*
Best Actress Katharine Hepburn in *On Golden Pond*

19**82**

Best Picture *Gandhi*
Best Actor Ben Kingsley in *Gandhi*
Best Actress Meryl Streep in *Sophie's Choice*

19**83**

Best Picture *Terms of Endearment*
Best Actor Robert Duvall in *Tender Mercies*
Best Actress Shirley MacLaine in *Terms of Endearment*

1984

Best Picture *Amadeus*
Best Actor F. Murray Abraham in *Amadeus*
Best Actress Sally Field in *Places in the Heart*

1985

Best Picture *Out of Africa*
Best Actor William Hurt in *Kiss of the Spider Woman*
Best Actress Geraldine Page in *The Trip to Bountiful*

1986

Best Picture *Platoon*
Best Actor Paul Newman in *The Color of Money*
Best Actress Marlee Matlin in *Children of a Lesser God*

1987

Best Picture *The Last Emperor*
Best Actor Michael Douglas in *Wall Street*
Best Actress Cher in *Moonstruck*

1988

Best Picture *Rain Man*
Best Actor Dustin Hoffman in *Rain Man*
Best Actress Jodie Foster in *The Accused*

1989

Best Picture *Driving Miss Daisy*
Best Actor Daniel Day-Lewis in *My Left Foot*
Best Actress Jessica Tandy in *Driving Miss Daisy*

These Flicks May or May Not Have Won Awards,
but They Were the

Top-Grossing Movies
of the '80s

1980 *Airplane!*
Any Which Way You Can
The Empire Strikes Back
9 to 5
Stir Crazy

1981 *Arthur*
Cannonball Run
On Golden Pond
Raiders of the Lost Ark
Stripes
Superman 2

1982 *E.T.: The Extra-Terrestrial*
An Officer and a Gentleman
Porky's
Rocky 3
Tootsie

1983 *Return of the Jedi*
Superman 3
Terms of Endearment
Trading Places
WarGames

1984 *Beverly Hills Cop*
Ghostbusters
Gremlins
Indiana Jones and the Temple of Doom
The Karate Kid

1985 *Back to the Future*
The Color Purple
Out of Africa
Rambo: First Blood, Part 2
Rocky 4

1986 *Crocodile Dundee*
The Karate Kid: Part 2
Platoon
Star Trek 4: The Voyage Home
Top Gun

1987 *Beverly Hills Cop 2*
Fatal Attraction
Good Morning, Vietnam
Lethal Weapon
Three Men and a Baby
The Untouchables

1988 *Coming to America*
Crocodile Dundee 2
Die Hard
Rain Man
Twins
Who Framed Roger Rabbit?

1989 *Batman*
Driving Miss Daisy
Ghostbusters 2
Honey, I Shrunk the Kids
Indiana Jones and the Last Crusade
Lethal Weapon 2
Look Who's Talking

John Hughes,
the Voice of a Generation of Adolescents

Sixteen Candles
(1984)

The Breakfast Club
(1985)

Weird Science
(1985)

Ferris Bueller's Day Off
(1986)

Planes, Trains & Automobiles
(1987)

She's Having a Baby
(1988)

Uncle Buck
(1989)

233 FILM

John Cusak:
Movie Boy of the Decade

Class (1983)

Grandview U.S.A. (1984)

Sixteen Candles (1984)

The Sure Thing (1985)

The Journey of Natty Gann (1985)

Better Off Dead (1985)

Stand By Me (1986)

One Crazy Summer (1986)

Hot Pursuit (1987)

Eight Men Out (1988)

Stars and Bars (1988)

Tapeheads (1989)

Fat Man and Little Boy (1989)

Elvis Stories (1989)

Say Anything (1989)

Molly Ringwald:
Movie Girl of the Decade

The Tempest (1982)

Packin' It In (1983)

Spacehunter: Adventures in the Forbidden Zone (1983)

Sixteen Candles (1984)

The Breakfast Club (1985)

P.K. and the Kid (1985)

Johnny Appleseed (1986)

Pretty in Pink (1986)

King Lear (1987)

The Pick-Up Artist (1987)

For Keeps (1988)

Fresh Horses (1988)

Gory to the Max:
Horror and Slasher Films

Bad Blood   Big Meat Eater

Bloodbath in Psycho Town   Blood Cult

Burial Ground

Cheerleader Camp   Children of the Corn

Child's Play   C.H.U.D.

Don't Go in the Woods

Firestarter   Evil Dead

Frightmare

Friday the 13th series

Hack O'Lantern   Halloween sequels

Hellraiser

Heathers

The Hidden   The Hitcher
         The Howling (Parts 1-5)
Keep My Grave Open
         Motel Hell   My Bloody Valentine
A Nightmare on Elm Street series
         The Offspring   Pet Sematary
Poltergeist   Pumpkinhead
Re-Animator   Scanners
The Shining
Silent Night, Deadly Night (Parts 1-3)
         The Toxic Avenger (Parts 1-3)
The Two Faces of Evil
                    Unsane

237 FILM

Sequel Whores of the '80s

Back to the Future (1985)
Back to the Future, Part 2 (1989)

Beverly Hills Cop (1984)
Beverly Hills Cop 2 (1987)

Black Stallion (1979)
The Black Stallion Returns (1983)

Breakin' (1984)
Breakin' 2: Electric Boogaloo (1984)

Caddyshack (1980)
Caddyshack 2 (1988)

Cannonball Run (1981)
Cannonball Run II (1984)

Cocoon (1985)
Cocoon: The Return (1988)

Conan the Barbarian (1982)
Conan the Destroyer (1984)

Death Wish 2 (1982)
Death Wish 3 (1985)

Evil Dead (1983)
└─────────────────● *Evil Dead 2: Dead by Dawn* (1987)

First Blood (1982)
          Rambo: First Blood, Part 2 (1985)
└─────────────● *Rambo 3* (1988)

Fletch (1985) ────────────────┐
     Fletch Lives (1989) ●──────┘

Friday the 13th (1980) ──────────────────────────────────┐
               Friday the 13th, Part 2 (1981)
          Friday the 13th, Part 3 (1982)
Friday the 13th, Part 4: The Final Chapter (1984)
               Friday the 13th, Part 5: A New Beginning (1985)
          Friday the 13th, Part 6: Jason Lives (1986)
Friday the 13th, Part 7: The New Blood (1988)
          Friday the 13th, Part 8: Jason Takes Manhattan (1989) ●──┘

Halloween 2: The Nightmare Isn't Over! (1981)
               Halloween 3: Season of the Witch (1982)
     Halloween 4: The Return of Michael Myers (1988)
└────────● *Halloween 5: The Revenge of Michael Myers* (1989)

Hellraiser (1987) ────────────┐
     Hellbound: Hellraiser II (1988) ●──┘

239
FILM

The Howling (1981)

Howling 2: Your Sister Is a Werewolf (1986)

Lethal Weapon (1987)

Lethal Weapon 2 (1989)

National Lampoon's Vacation (1983)

National Lampoon's European Vacation (1985)

National Lampoon's Christmas Vacation (1989)

A Nightmare on Elm Street (1984)

A Nightmare on Elm Street 2: Freddy's Revenge (1985)

A Nightmare on Elm Street 3: Dream Warriors (1987)

A Nightmare on Elm Street 4: Dream Master (1988)

A Nightmare on Elm Street 5: Dream Child (1989)

Police Academy (1984)

Police Academy 2: Their First Assignment (1985)

Police Academy 3: Back in Training (1986)

Police Academy 4: Citizens on Patrol (1987)

Police Academy 5: Assignment Miami Beach (1988)

Police Academy 6: City Under Siege (1989)

Poltergeist (1982)

Poltergeist 2: The Other Side (1986)

Poltergeist 3 (1988)

Psycho 2 (1983)
└──────────────────► ● *Psycho 3* (1986)

Revenge of the Nerds (1984) ─────────────────────┐
      Revenge of the Nerds 2: Nerds in Paradise (1987) ● ──┘

Rocky III (1982) ┐
    └─● *Rocky IV* (1986)

Silent Night, Deadly Night (1984) ───────────────┐
     Silent Night, Deadly Night 2 (1987)
Silent Night, Deadly Night 3: Better Watch Out! (1989) ● ──┘

Sleepaway Camp (1983)
│   *Sleepaway Camp 2: Unhappy Campers* (1988)
└──● *Sleepaway Camp 3: Teenage Wasteland* (1989)

Star Trek: The Motion Picture (1980) ─────────────┐
   Star Trek II: The Wrath of Khan (1982)
        Star Trek III: The Search for Spock (1984)
   Star Trek IV: The Voyage Home (1986)
Star Trek V: The Final Frontier (1989) ● ──────────────┘

Superman 2 (1980)
│   *Superman 3* (1983)
└──● *Superman 4: The Quest for Peace* (1987)

241 FILM

animals, comedians, athletes,
supermodels, news anchors,
criminals making headlines,
politicians, international
figures, marriages, deaths,
people we loved to hate . . .

PEOPLE of the '80s

PEOPLE

Don't Have a Cow!: Animals from the '80s

Bear [monkey from *B.J. and the Bear*]

Black Beauty

Benji

Boomer

Brandon

Bubbles [Michael Jackson's monkey]

Charlotte and Wilbur

Clyde [the orangutan from Eastwood movies]

Cujo

Dinky [National Lampoon's Vacation dog left on bumper]

Flash [basset from *The Dukes of Hazzard*]

Freeway [Hart to Hart]

Flipper

Frogger

Hooch

Jabba the Hut

Kermit the Frog

KoKo, the signing gorilla

Millie
[President Bush's dog]

Miss Piggy

Morris the Cat

RCA dog paired with a puppy

Riki-Tiki-Tavi

Shamu, the killer whale

"Sit, Ubu, sit. Good dog!"
[Black Dog Productions]

Snakes from *Raiders of the Lost Ark*

Spiders from *Arachnophobia*

Spuds McKenzie

Toonces the Cat

Winnie-the-Pooh

Yoda

245 PEOPLE

DELIRIOUS AND RAW COMEDIANS
We'd Try to Catch on Cable

Louie Anderson
Roseanne Barr
John Belushi
Sandra Bernhard
Elayne Boosler
John Candy
George Carlin
Dana Carvy
Andrew Dice Clay
Billy Crystal
Jane Curtain
Ellen Degeneres

Bobcat Goldthwait
Pee-Wee Herman
Sam Kinison
Richard Lewis
Jon Lovitz
Bill Maher
Howie Mandel
Steve Martin
Dennis Miller
Larry Miller
Eddie Murphy
Rosie O'Donnell
Kevin Pollack
Paula Poundstone

247 PEOPLE

Richard Pryor
Gilda Radner
Paul Reiser
Joan Rivers
Rita Rudner
Jerry Seinfeld
Garry Shandling
Martin Short
Sinbad
Judy Tenuta
Gene Wilder
Steven Wright
Robert Wuhl

Athletes Who Felt the Thrill of Victory and the Agony of Defeat

Kareem Abdul-Jabbar

Andre Agassi

Marcus Allen

Evelyn Ashford

Boris Becker

Larry Bird

Wade Boggs

Brian Boitano

Bjorn Borg

Terry Bradshaw

George Brett

Earl Campbell

249 PEOPLE

Jennifer Capriati

Dwight Clark

Bart Conner

Jim Craig

Jimmy Connors

Eric Dickerson

Stefan Edberg

John Elway

Mike Eruzione

Julius Erving

Chris Evert

Patrick Ewing

A. J. Foyt

Doug Flutie

Mitch Gaylord

Dwight Gooden

Wayne Gretzky

Florence Griffith-Joyner

Dorothy Hamill

Scott Hamilton

Thomas Hearns

Eric Heiden Bo Jackson

Magic Johnson

Michael Jordan

Jackie Joyner-Kersee

Greg LeMond

Ivan Lendl

Sugar Ray Leonard

Carl Lewis

James Lofton

251 PEOPLE

Ronnie Lott

Greg Louganis

Dan Marino

John McEnroe

Jim McMahon

Mark Messier

Joe Montana

Edwin Moses

Martina Navratilova

Jack Nicklaus

Brian Orser

Walter Payton

William "The Refrigerator" Perry

Kyle Petty

Mary Lou Retton

Jerry Rice

Pete Rose

Barry Sanders

Leon Spinks

Roger Staubach

Lyn St. James

Lawrence Taylor

Vinny Testaverde

Joe Theismann

Debi Thomas

Mike Tyson

Fernando Valenzuela

Jim Valvano

Tom Watson

Frank White

Katerina Witt

253 PEOPLE

Bodacious Supermodels

Christie **Brinkley**

Lynda **Carter**

Phoebe **Cates**

Cindy **Crawford**

Farrah **Fawcett**

Jerry **Hall**

Rachel
H u n t e r

Iman

Kathy
I r e l a n d

Kate
J a c k s o n

Grace
J o n e s

Cheryl
L a d d

Kelly
L e B r o c k

255
PEOPLE

Andie
M a c D o w e l l

Elle
M a c p h e r s o n

Julianne
P h i l l i p s

Paulina
P o r i z k o v a

Isabella
R o s s e l l i n i

Cheryl
T i e g s

Heather
T h o m a s

Noteworthy
News Anchors

Tom Brokaw
Connie Chung
Katie Couric
Walter Cronkite
Sam Donaldson
Charles Gibson
Bryant Gumbel
Peter Jennings
Ted Koppel
Joan Lunden
Bill Moyers
Roger Mudd
Deborah Norville
Jane Pauley
Dan Rather
Barbara Walters

257 PEOPLE

BUST

People Whose Crimes Made Headlines

Jim Bakker

Bob Berdella
(Kansas City store owner who held men in his basement and tortured them)

Ivan Boesky

Ted Bundy

Mark David Chapman
(killed John Lennon)

Jeffrey Dahmer

John DeLorean

Jimmy Etheride
(infected more than fifty children in Texas and Mexico with AIDS)

John Wayne Gacy

Ed Gein

Bernhard Goetz
(shot subway youths)

Richard Grissolm

Fawn Hall

Patty Hearst

Reverend Gary Heidnik
(Philadelphia minister convicted of rape, murder, kidnapping,
and forced cannibalism)

John Hinckley Jr.

James Huberty
(fired on customers at a San Ysidoro, California, McDonald's,
killing twenty-one)

Lee Iacocca

Charles Keating
(responsible for notorious savings and loan failures)

Charles Manson

Michael Milken
(financial criminal, junk bonds)

Oliver North

Manuel Noriega

Richard Ramirez, the Night Stalker

Wayne Williams
(convicted of a string of murders of mostly young, black boys in Atlanta)

Politicians:
THE LEADERS OF OUR NATION

James Baker

Marion Barry

Lloyd Bentsen Jr.

Joseph Biden

Sonny Bono

Pat Buchanan

George Bush

Jimmy Carter

Alan Cranston

Mario Cuomo

Bob Dole

Michael Dukakis

Clint Eastwood

Geraldine Ferraro

Richard Gephardt

Rudolph Giuliani

Alexander Haig

Gary Hart

Jesse Jackson

Jack Kemp

Ted Kennedy

Russell Long

Ed Meese

Walter Mondale

Sam Nunn

John Poindexter

Dan Quayle

Ronald Reagan

Pat Robertson

Pat Schroeder

George Schultz

Caspar Weinberger

International Figures

Corazon Aquino ■ Yasser Arafat
Fidel Castro ■ François Duvalier (Papa Doc)
Mu'ammar Gadhafi
Mikhail ■ Gorbachev
Ayatollah Khomeini ■ Nelson Mandela
Ferdinand and Emelda Marcos
François Mitterrand ■ Manuel Noriega
Augusto Pinochet ■ Princess Diana
Princess Stephanie ■ Anwar Sadat
Margaret Thatcher ■ Bishop Desmond Tutu

Till Death Do You Part:
Memorable Marriages Made in the '80s

Prince Andrew

Sarah Ferguson

Barbara Walters

Prince Charles

Lady Diana

Merv Adelson

Tracey Pollen

Michael J. Fox

Billy Joel

Christie Brinkley

Melanie Griffith

Don Johnson

Tommy Lee

Heather Locklear

Tatum O'Neal

John McEnroe

Ric Ocasek

Paulina Porizkova

Burt Reynolds
💜
Loni Anderson

Caroline Kennedy
💜
Edwin Schlossberg

Madonna
💜
Sean Penn

Carrie Fisher
💜
Paul Simon

Arnold Schwarzenegger
💜
Maria Shriver

Julianne Phillips
💜
Bruce Springsteen

Valerie Bertinelli
💜
Eddie Van Halen

Mike Tyson
💜
Robin Givens

Bruce Willis
💜
Demi Moore

265
PEOPLE

People Who Departed
Before Seeing the '80s Through

Ansel Adams (1984)

(1986) **V. C. Andrews**

Fred Astaire
(1987)

Lucille Ball (1989)

Eddie Bauer
(1986)

(1982) **John Belushi**

Irving Berlin
(1989)

(1989) **Mel Blanc**

Leonid Brezhnev
(1982)

James Cagney
(1986)

Karen Carpenter (1983)

(1989) Salvador Dali

Bette Davis (1989)

Jack Dempsey
(1983)

Divine (1988)

(1982) Henry Fonda

Dian Fossey
(1985)

Indira Gandhi
(1984)

Marvin Gaye
(1984)

(1987) Jackie Gleason

267
PEOPLE

(1986) **Cary Grant**

Rita Hayworth
(1987)
Alfred Hitchcock (1980)

Rock Hudson
(1985)
John Huston (1987)

Andy Kaufman (1984)

(1982) **Grace Kelly**

Ray Kroc (1984)

Louis L'Amour
(1988)

Meyer Lansky (1983)

John Lennon
(1980)

Liberace (1987)

Roger Maris (1985)

(1980) Steve McQueen

Ricky Nelson
(1985)

Arthur Nielsen (1980)

Sir Lawrence Olivier
(1989)

(1988) Roy Orbison

Jesse Owens
(1980)

Leroy "Satchel" Paige
(1982)

(1986)

Marlin Perkins

(1989) Gilda Radner

269 PEOPLE

(1981) **Anwar al-Sadat**

Jean-Paul Sartre
(1980)

(1980)**Peter Sellers**

Gloria Swanson(1983)

(1982) **Bess Truman**

Andy Warhol(1987)

Orson Welles (1985)

Mae West
(1980)

(1983)
Tennessee Williams

Dennis Wilson
(1983)

Natalie Wood(1981)

We Absolutely Loved
to Hate . . .

Roseanne Barr

Alexis Carrington on *Dynasty* (Joan Collins)

Jimmy Carter and/or his brother Billy

Mark David Chapman for taking away John Lennon

J. R. Ewing on *Dallas*
(Larry Hagman)

Mu'ammar Gadhafi, Libyan leader

John Wayne Gacy

The grouch who was always behind the "hauntings" on *Scooby-Doo*

Leona Helmsley

John Hinckley Jr.

Ayatollah Khomeini

Freddy Krueger

Lester Maddox, the racist governor of Georgia

Imelda Marcos and all her shoes

John McEnroe

Menudo

New Kids on the Block

Manuel Noriega

Oliver North

Sinéad O'Connor

Ozzy Osbourne

"Patient Zero," malicious early sufferer of AIDS
who purposely spread the virus

Richard Ramirez, the Night Stalker

Nancy Reagan

Geraldo Rivera

Pete Rose

Erno Rubik, the inventor of the Rubik's Cube

Richard Simmons

The Soviet Union

Rick Springfield
(only the men hated him)

George Steinbrenner

Donald Trump